WHOLENESS LOST
AND
WHOLENESS REGAINED

D1606121

SUNY Series in Buddhist Studies
Matthew Kapstein, Editor

WHOLENESS LOST
AND
WHOLENESS REGAINED

*Forgotten Tales of Individuation
from Ancient Tibet*

Foreword by
David Michael Levin

HERBERT V. GUENTHER

STATE UNIVERSITY OF NEW YORK PRESS

Published by
State University of New York Press, Albany

© 1994   State University of New York

For information, address State University of New York Press,
State University Plaza, Albany, N.Y., 12246

Production by Cathleen Collins
Marketing by Dana Yanulavich

Library of Congress Cataloging-in-Publication Data

Guenther, Herbert V.
    Wholeness lost and wholeness regained : forgotten tales of
individuation from ancient Tibet / Herbert Guenther : foreword by
David Michael Levin.
        p.   cm. — (SUNY series in Buddhist studies)
    Includes bibliographical references and index.
    ISBN 0–7914–1989–4. — ISBN 0–7914–1990–8 (pbk.)
    1. Rdzogs-chen (Rñin-ma-pa). 2. Spiritual life—Buddhism.
3. Individuation (Philosophy) I. Title. II. Series.
BQ7662.4.G767   1994
294.3'444—dc20   93–27380
                                                         CIP

10 9 8 7 6 5 4 3 2 1

To
Ilse, as always,
and to
Jeanette and Mariana,
in particular

Contents

Foreword

In a journal entry for June 21, 1852, Henry David Thoreau wrote: "The perception of beauty is a moral test."[1] A test, he meant, of character—a test of character, moreover, not only in its ethical formation, but also in its spiritual vocation, that dimension of human existence in which we put into practice a commitment to cultivate our capacity for openness and wholeness. In the rDzogs-chen tradition of Buddhism that has flourished in Tibet, the cultivation of this capacity is the essence of growth and maturity. It is, indeed, at the very heart of the enlightenment process.

The "openness" in question, here, is our openness to what is other: different, outside, and beyond us, even absolutely other, different beyond measure. But this openness is also— for such are the ways of the spirit—an openness to what is already, and has always been, precisely ourselves: an openness, therefore, to *being* ourselves, being true to ourselves. But who are we? What kind of being are we? Do we know? Do we really know ourselves?

If we are not necessarily, and as a matter of essence, the self-contained, self-sufficient, self-grounded, self-centered individuals that our modern culture has long imagined, then perhaps openness in the sense of being true to ourselves does not mean growing up in obedience to a fixed, pre-existent, pre-determined essence or nature, but means, rather, understanding our inherence in the world, understanding the dynamics of our interdependence in relation to other beings, and indeed in relation to the world, the multidimensional matrix within which we exist, as a whole. Thus, being true to ourselves would involve being true, being open, to all that is *other* in relation to ourselves. It would mean extending the reach and range of our experience, extending our natural capacity for perception, sensibility, compassion, and intelligence to *include* what is different, even radically different, from ourselves: extending ourselves, and to the limit, perhaps even to the point where the conventional boundaries that, with the support of society, we have constructed to defend the ground and center of our being, are breached and forever shattered.

The spiritual development of character also involves wholeness. The desire, or say *need*, for wholeness is what motivates our openness. What, then, is called for in the cultivation of our capacity for "wholeness"? There are many conceptions of wholeness. However, most of them base wholeness on a principle of exclusion, a principle of delimitation. Wholeness then becomes a function of our defensiveness: defensiveness rather than adventure, anxiety rather than joy, inhibition rather than freedom, repetition rather than experimentation and growth. Such wholeness is accordingly achieved only by closure—and the price for this security is extremely high. But here, in the two ancient texts that Herbert Guenther has translated, the "wholeness" in question is a condition that depends, instead, on a principle of alterity, a principle of difference: our openness in relation to what is other. Although wholeness motivates openness, it is this openness that makes wholeness possible. For wholeness is possible only insofar as individuation becomes a way of participating in the *whole* of being, a way of integrating our individual identity into being *as* a whole, a way of identifying ourselves *with* the whole. And this is a process that requires us to experience ourselves, not as self-contained, self-sufficient, essentially independent beings, but rather as beings whose lives are intertwined with the lives and histories of all other beings—intertwined with the living and the dead, the sentient and the nonsentient, the present and the absent. We are, in a word, essentially interdependent. Thus, it is in learning to practice this interdependence in relation to all beings that we find our way to wholeness.

Beauty, it is said, is in the eye of the beholder. The way most people understand this saying, it encourages, and even legitimates, complacency. Beauty is relativized: you see things your way, I see them my way. But suppose that we resist this common interpretation. What if we take the saying as a solicitation, challenging us to cultivate, to develop, our capacity to see beauty—see it, for example, where we could not see it before? What does it take to see beauty where others cannot see it? What does it take to see beauty where before I saw nothing? I take Thoreau's remark to be reminding us that perception is a capacity, that this capacity can be cultivated and developed, and that this work on ourselves— with ourselves—is a process that involves the formation of character. What, for example, is the character of our vision? What is the character of our sensibility? Of what are we capable? Do we know?

In *The Politics of Experience*, R. D. Laing observed that, "If our experience is destroyed, our behavior will be destructive."[2] Our experience is being destroyed whenever its reality is not valued, not respected. It is also being destroyed whenever it is not cultivated, not given the attention it needs in order to grow and flourish. The moment of enlightenment may come in the flash of an instant, but it always depends on prior experiential work, processes of learning that *continue* to engage us—and indeed to test us—in the life that comes after this moment.

The Tibetan texts that Dr. Guenther has translated here, texts for which he has provided a commentary of incalculable value, are charming, but also demanding. They address us in a symbolic, allegorical language rooted in years of reflective cultivated experience; and, although they can certainly be read simply as narratives, their allegorical metaphorics carry very deep spiritual meaning, demanding of us a corresponding commitment to undergo the necessary experiential work.

Now, there is, in the West, a method for working with our experience: a method that may bear some surprising fruit when used in our reading of the present book. The method to which I am referring is hermeneutical phenomenology. This method values and respects the reality of our experience just as we actually live it. But it also values and respects the *depths* of our experience—its dimensionality. Some people live entirely on, and from, the surface of their experience. But our experience is deeper than we know, more than we understand: there is always a potential greater than we have realized and actualized. Hermeneutical phenomenology works with the great potential, the latent as well as the manifest, encouraging us to explore the true dimensionality of our experience.

How should we understand this truth—the truth that such hermeneutical phenomenology brings to light? According to the paradigm of truth dominant in our culture, truth is a question of correctness: the correspondence between a state of affairs—an experience of suffering, for example—and its symbolic representation. The sentence "The snowfall here is heavy" is thus a true representation if and only if the snowfall here is actually heavy. But human experience is not a simple state of affairs. Whereas the snowfall here either is or is not heavy, and there is a simple fact of the matter, our experience is permeated by a living awareness, very deep and very complex. In order to work with our experience—work, that is, in a way that is true to its life, its reflective intricacy, its complexity and dimensionality—hermeneutical phenomenology must work with a different paradigm of truth.

The "truth" that figures in hermeneutical phenomenology is a process of disclosure. In the context of discourse, the difference between truth as correctness and truth as disclosure is constitutive of the difference between statements and the articulations of poetry, a difference, therefore, between monotone assertions with univocal meaning and polyphonic utterances with multiple meanings, conveyed through resonances, reverberations, and echoes. In the context of vision, the difference between these two models of truth is constitutive of the difference between the detached gaze and neutral observations of a spectator and the gaze of the participant, touched and moved by what she is given to see. Only the latter gaze is open to the whole. Only the latter gaze, rooted in its felt sense of beings and moved by its felt sense of the interdependency of all beings, could enjoy a realization of wholeness.

I have said the the two texts which Dr. Guenther has chosen to write about are allegorical stories. They are stories of experience, but their truth is encoded in the language of metaphors. And as the etymology of the word "metaphor" tells us, a living metaphor is a word that transports us, carries us, moves us, takes us from an old and familiar meaning to the surprise of a meaning that is different, new. Consequently, the truth that these stories have to offer is a truth that can be rewardingly realized only by a reading that is hermeneutically phenomenological. What this means is that, in order to realize their truth, readers must *participate* in their unfolding. We must allow ourselves to be deeply touched and moved by the experiential movement of the metaphor: we must allow ourselves to be taken wheresoever they would move us. We must entrust ourselves to the light in their vision.

The metaphors in the Tibetan texts are not mere embellishments, mere decorations. They carry experiential meaning; they refer us to dimensions of meaning with which they are familiar, and attempt to communicate in a way that will enjoin us to work with our own experience, so that we may get to know these dimensions and engage them for ourselves. These metaphors are meant to effect *transformations* in our experience of existence. In contrast to the truths recognized by positivism, the truths of these metaphors are neither ready-made nor the function of some state of affairs, some condition, that precedes them, that already exists in the world. Instead, these metaphors *make* themselves true by changing us. They are true only to the extent that they succeed in soliciting our reflective awareness and bring about a transformation in our experience. Therefore, they are not constatives; that is, they are not true in the way that statements or assertions are true, mirroring, or corresponding to, some already existing *state* of reality. Rhetorically considered, they are *performative* utterances, making themselves true, rather, in the ways, and to the extent that, they can engage us, can stimulate and motivate us, to work *with* them in exploring the dimensions of our experience. Such metaphors assume that our experience is a living process, not a state. And, as allegorical, they assume that the dimensionality of this process can be opened up, exposing us to that which is other. This kind of process is called "hermeneutical," because it is neither a process of pure creation, pure self-invention *ex nihilo*, nor a process of mere discovery, simply acknowledging what has been present all along. One might say, perhaps, that it is rather a process in which a certain experiencing potential is recognized, worked with, and developed—except that even this formulation lends itself to a metaphysical interpretation that reifies the dynamics of the potential, conceiving it to be in a state of full presence. This interpretation could only, however, be unfortunate, because it would entail a process of individuation in which our experiencing has been foreclosed to the openness of existence, the very dimensionality of wholeness into which these maieutic texts are attempting to draw us.

Readers who open their hearts to these precious narratives of individuation, mindfully participating in the experiential processes that Dr. Guenther so lucidly interprets, will find in the reading of these stories that rarest of joys—a fulfillment that a can only come from learning the simple poetry of living deeply.

David Michael Levin

Department of Philosophy
Northwestern University
Evanston, Illinois

Notes

1. See B. Torrey, and F. Allen, eds., *The Journal of Henry David Thoreau*, vol. II (New York: Dover, 1906), p. 43.

2. R. D. Laing, *The Politics of Experience* (New York: Ballantine Books, 1967), p. 28.

Preface

This book is intended for all those who are interested in the perennial task of coming to know themselves "holistically" in a non-reductionist and non-divisible manner. Such a quest for wholeness is intimately and intricately intertwined with a phenomenological exploration of the dynamics of psychic life as it expresses itself in images as symbolic descriptions of itself and in this self-presentation remain a challenge for further explorations. In this sense, they have little to do with philosophical speculation that inevitably ends in a theoretical construct from which, carrion-like, all life has been excluded. Viewed from another angle, this book reflects my own interest in a person's growth, as the case may be, into his or her humanity that is not gender-reducible; and also it must not to be confused with some pathological ego-identity. Rather, such growth is tantamount to an expanding of the boundaries of self-knowledge involving intellectual and emotional integrity so sadly lacking, if not to say, deliberately suppressed, repressed, and destroyed in the contemporary scene by ready-made answers to questions that have never been asked by the vociferous fundamentalist-dogmatists of every provenance.

This interest, in good part, was aroused by my specialization in Indian (Brahmanical and Buddhist) and Tibetan (mostly Buddhist) thought based on my avid reading of Indian and Tibetan literary works (in the original languages, of course) as well as by a rapt contemplation of the visual arts as their quite literally tangible expressions. Whether we look at Indian sculptures in all their sensuous and often sensual richness or at Tibetan paintings in which the humanly divine or, what is the same, the divinely human figures have been resolved into fluid lines there is an intense quality about them that seems to lend added significance to Johann Wolfgang von Goethe's dictum *Sinnlichkeit ist Sittlichkeit* (sensibility implies morality)[1]—morality being spirituality's dynamics working *within* and *through* us as our capacity for being sensuously and emotionally (spiritually) affected. In so being simultaneously sensuous and spiritual the meaning of Indian and Tibetan art is accessible only to and appreciable by the beholder's immediate experience; it is quickly lost as soon as it is misplaced and distorted into objective postulates or subjective (ego-logically prompted) affectations. So it is with the quest for wholeness or, as C. G. Jung has called it, the "process of individuation" that is neither some intellectual (deadly reductionist) enterprise, nor some sentimental flight into an ultimately sterile phantasy. Individuation must be experienced in order to be comprehended and that means that, in the present case, what started as a mere interest, in the course of time, intensified by Martin Heidegger's and Maurice Merleau-Ponty's phenomenological and C. G. Jung's psychological probings, culminating in the latter's vision of humanity's spiritual integration, soon turned into a joyous and active engagement reflecting, on my part, an elective affinity with the emphasis on light that, as the reader will notice, is the leitmotiv of the stories in the present study.

While stories about individuation are widespread in the folk tales of many countries, they have practically disappeared from the Tibetan scene for reasons not far to seek. The literary form most suitable for depicting the individuation theme is an allegory that carries a second meaning along with the surface story. In the Buddhist context, the use of allegory (*brda'*) with its wealth of sensuously spiritual and/or spiritually sensuous symbols is found only in the older (*rnying-ma*) tradition in works associated with the enigmatic figure of Padmasambhava and his circle of followers. From what we can gather from his own writings he was too independent a thinker as to fit into the emergent intellectualistic trend of the new (*gsar-ma*) tradition that became ever more concerned with upholding ideologically restrictive myths and models, rather than with furthering an experiential understanding of an individual's striving for wholeness. Hence, the older works were rigorously excluded from the standard version of Buddhist texts compiled and approved by the new sectarian mood that swept Tibet because they did not conform to the demands set by its orthodoxy and, as a consequence, they fell into oblivion. Therefore, the two stories of this study are "forgotten" tales in the strict sense of the word.

The plan of this book is such that it can be read by anyone whose main interest is in the unfolding of a story and therefore might prefer to skip its documentation in the notes. It can also be read by anyone whose interest extends further into the background against which the stories were told and whose tremendous wealth they "reveal." In this case, the notes are indispensable. Needless to say, they are based on the undeservedly neglected and mostly forgotten sources of the "older" tradition, here presented in the English language for the first time.

This book owes a great deal to my life and to those under whom I have studied as well as to those with whom I am still working.

Special thanks are due to David Michael Levin for invaluable comments and for his willingness to write the Foreword; to Allan Combs and Stanley Krippner for their helpful suggestions; to Brian Newman and Reinhold Ortlepp for drawing the diagrams. I am also grateful to Mariana Neves for her supportive interest in the book's growth and to my daughter Edith Kimbell for her polishing the draft through her writing skills. To the editorial staff of SUNY Press I am particularly grateful for the sensitive care [he/she/they] bestowed on the editing and final production.

Last, but not least, I have to thank my wife Ilse for more than what can be expressed in words.

Notes

1. The German word *Sinnlichkeit* is highly ambivalent: it may connote "sensuality," usually and reductively understood as carnal (sexual) gratifi-

cation; primarily, however, it relates to what affects and/or appeals to the senses, especially, aesthetically. For obvious reasons as well as for the encouragement by David Michael Levin, I have avoided the common run-of-the-mill translations of the German classics and, unless stated otherwise, all translations from German are mine.

Introduction

The two stories that form the basis of the following study have been selected from one of the oldest extant texts belonging to what has become known as the rDzogs-chen tradition in Buddhist thought.[1] By the time this text was set up in its present form, the rDzogs-chen tradition had already passed through several stages in its development and was still evolving. In order to appreciate the richness of this essentially spiritual tradition and its reflection in basically elucidatory stories, it is necessary to draw attention to some of the more important ingredients that went into the formation of this line of thought that, as far as Buddhist thinking is concerned, is quite unique. The tradition can be traced back to the early centuries of the present era and the internal evidence points to an origin at a time of intense intellectual activity in a region where Hellenistic ideas (Pythagorean-Platonic[2] and Neoplatonic-Gnostic)[3] and Buddhist ideas (Indian-Buddhist and Chinese-Buddhist) met and certainly had an impact on each other, even if, finally, each thought system followed its own momentum in dealing with the ideas it encountered to build its respective model of reality. Thus, one set of ideas, the Hellenistic one, stressed the philosophical-speculative (rational) aspect and, by necessity, remained structure-oriented, resulting in a vertically and rigidly hierarchically determined order of the universe that stayed intimately connected with the Limited (*peras*) as contrasted with the Unlimited (*apeiron*) of which Plato had spoken as the Indeterminate Dyad; the other, the Buddhist one, stressed the contemplative-experiential (mystic) aspect and, in being process-oriented, conceived of structures as *process structures*[4] that involved both vertical (hierarchically co-ordinated) and horizontal (field-like) dimensions.

This difference in perspective may be elucidated by quoting from the outstanding representatives of both. In the Hellenistic framework, Pythagoras and Plotinus attached paramount importance to the notion of the "One." But whether Pythagoras and the Pythagoreans believed in the One as existing above the Monad and the Dyad, as claimed by Eudorus of Alexandria, is doubtful.[5] For Plotinus, the One is the eternal source of all being of which in his *Enneads*[6] he says: "Generative of all, The Unity is none of all, neither thing nor quantity nor quality nor intellect nor soul."[7]

rDzogs-chen thinkers, for whom the universe is not only intrinsically "intelligent," but also a self-organizing whole of intensities, too, refer to what superficially looks like *a* or *the* One (*nyag-gcig*). However, they do not mean by it some entity or other set absolute,[8] rather they attempt to convey by it the fusion of two contrary notions into a single dynamic one expressing, if we may say so, the experiencer's psychophysical continuum. This becomes evident in the frequently used combination *thig-le nyag-gcig*, a term that defies any simple translation and may best be paraphrased as "the whole's uniquely autopoietic dynamics."[9] One of its earliest hermeneutical interpretations is found in the *Byang-chub-tu sems skyob-pa*[10] and runs as follows:

thig　means unmoved, invariant, unerring, straight, dissociated from conceptual proliferations;

le　means the totality of the concrete, widely distributed, arising as anything;

nyag　means profound and subtle and hence difficult to fathom;

gcig　means the continuum of (the ternary relationship between an (objective) cognitive domain, a (subjective) mind, and an (autocatalytic) self,[11] in whichever way one may think and speak of it.

Similarly Śrīsiṃha states in his *Ye-shes gsang-ba sgron-me*:[12]

thig　means invariance, (one's) self-reflexive mind[13]; that is, the unborn;

le   means the distribution (of the concrete), radiating in
(the whole's) homogeneity/self-consistency;[14]
The unity (of *thig* and *le*) means oneness (*gcig*).[15]

The final quotation comes from Padmasambhava's magnum opus, the *sPros-bral don-gsal*:

> Since apart from (the whole's) auto-presencing—there is
> no allo-presencing—the (whole's) energy/intensity "stuff"
> remains invariant, the coming-to-presence (of the phenomenal world) is (the whole's) uniquely autopoietic
> dynamics (*thig-le nyag-gcig*) radiating in its absolute auto-
> presencing.[16]

Special attention should be paid to the whole's auto-presencing in what is experienced as the phenomenal world in whose actual presence the experiencer plays an important role by "interpreting" what "lights up."[17] Speaking of the whole's auto-presencing as an auto-dynamic lighting-up is a phenomenologically accurate description of an inner psychic process experienced as having a light quality that is the observable facet of a pre-existent light carrying with it the potential-for-being and expressing itself as a probability distribution.

Another example that illustrates not only the close connection, but also the tremendous difference that existed between early rDzogs-chen thought and Hellenistic-Gnostic ideas which spread throughout Asia Minor and Central Asia, is how each line of thought dealt with the idea of the world's origin, that is, the world in which we live. Broadly speaking, the Gnostics who could never rid themselves of their Hellenistic legacy of a static cosmos, even if it had emanated from a hypothetical One with which it nevertheless contrasted, and the Judaeo-Christian idea of a creator, whether he be good or evil, were forced to conceive of the world as being something that had been "created," and thus they remained caught in a dualism that reflected their restrictively rational approach to the question of Being. By contrast, the rDzogs-chen thinkers grounded in a different culture and being process-oriented in their thinking could not but conceive of the origin of the world as a self-organizing process whose success or failure was a matter of comprehension or incomprehension on the part of the experiencer as an integral aspect of this process.

In reading Padmasambhava's writings, we are struck by both the similarity of his search, if not so say, his experience of the No, the non-being and non-existent that language is powerless to interpret, with the statements by Basilides, *Basileides* in Greek, the foremost Gnostic thinker (85–145 C.E.), who according to Hippolytos (d. 236 C.E.) had spoken of a primal "non-existent god," and the originality of Padmasambhava's own thinking with its rich repertoire of analogies as an aid to facilitate an understanding, not as a means to prove anything.

Being, the whole and as such, figuratively speaking, the ground for all that is to be and by implication the ground of all that is, is for Padmasambhava, as it is in modern times for Martin Heidegger, not *a* being or *a* ground; rather it is, if this copula is at all applicable, itself a "ground-that-is-not."[18] Thus, whatever may be said about it can only be a suggestion to make the listener experience for himself what is so intimated. Padmasambhava lists four analogies to elucidate the dynamics, vastness, richness, and preciousness of Being: ice forming on a lake, arable land, a king's treasure, and gold.[19] He then distinguishes between four nuances or functions of Being, the first of which he calls "Being-as-Dasein."[20] By this he neither means that it is some place or space, nor that it is somewhere or in space; what he wants us to understand by it he expresses in words appealing immediately to our imagination and feelings:

> When ice is forming on a lake
> [It becomes impossible to say what is ice and what is
> water][21]
> (Eventually) there will be be no furrows and their
> edges, no highs and lows, and no ridges and ravines.[22]

(The frozen lake) will (ultimately) continue in the
smoothness of its consistency with itself and
everything else.[23]

It is precisely these things-that-are-not that make up our
world of things[24] that in spite of what may be felt as its irrealization remains quite real and it is Being-as-placement that
allows the things-that-are-not to occupy space according to
their intensities. This paradox does not warrant the assumption that the world we are and live in is an illusion.[25] This
world of ours is quite "real," though it may not be what it is
claimed to be by the reductionist rationalist who merely does
not know better because of his limited understanding.

Closely related to Being in its function of providing a
space for the things-that-are-not, is its "world-spanning."[26]
The standard analogy Padmasambhava uses to elucidate what
is meant by this aspect of Being is "oil pervading sesame
seeds," and its world-spanning function is, as he goes on to
elaborate, noticeable in the loftiest realms of spiritual wakefulness as well as in the deepest layers and darkest regions of
spiritual blindness. Padmasambhava's assessment of Being in
its dual function of *Da*-sein and world-spanning allows us,
from a strictly experiential perspective, to say that we (and
our world of which we are an integral aspect) are not *in*
space, as Blaise Pascal (1623–1662) wanted to make us
believe, but *are* space.

Similar to the intimate connection that exists between
"Being-as-Dasein" and "Being-as-world-spanning" as giving
rise to our idea of space, is the connection between the
remaining two functions of Being that give rise to our idea of
time. The first of these two latter functions is termed "Being-
as-movement."[27] There is according to Padmasambhava first
a pre-initial Being-as-Dasein in which a proto-initial Being
stirs in which, in turn, an originary or primal Being stirs and
moves into what is to be Being's eigenstate or Being-as-such
that then moves into the world-spanning Being we have
already encountered in connection with Being-as-Dasein.[28]

In this world-spanning Being, the "wind"[29] of Being's originary or primal presencing begins to blow and erupts out of
its latency into a "gusty" actuality whereby, as we might say,
space now becomes space-time.

Space-time, in Padmasambhava's words the combination
of the "wind" of Being's originary or primal presencing and
its "gusty" actuality or, as we would say, the intensification
of the former into the latter, marks what he calls "Being-as-
fundamental-forces."[30] Eventually these forces will become
the building blocks of the physical aspect of ours and our
world that marks a reversible end-phase in a process of radiation-dominated energy thereby becoming matter-dominated
energy. Here the idea of "energy" is introduced by Padmasambhava himself and according to him this energy in
itself is indistinguishable from what has been referred to (not
"defined") as "Being/ground/the whole" except for its
emphasizing the dynamic character of wholeness that is
"felt" by us as a pervasive energizing force. Though in what it
is in itself it is unmoved and unmoving, its creative dynamics
is marked by a lighting-up that "branches out" as rays of
intense light.[31] The implication is that we are not only space-
time beings, but also more importantly luminous beings.
And just as the light that we are in its spreading or branching
out may be broken up into specific luminosities of its own
making, the light's rays, so in moving away from our source
(the wholeness that is Being) into individual beings, we may
become quite literally lost. But the memory of the source
lingers on and we yearn to return to it (be it only for a while
to gain new strength). In speaking of this return of the "scattered" light to its "unitary" source, Padmasambhava employs
one of the most touching images—a child meeting its mother
again. Thus, he explicitly states:[32]

> When the lighting-up of (Being's) creative dynamics
>   into (its) spiritually cognitive capacity, (its) child,
>   meets
> The proto-initial energy, (its) mother,

The indivisibility of mother and child, a meeting and
   fusing,
Takes up its (legitimate) dwelling in (what is Being's)
   non-origination and is sealed by (Being's)
   invariance.[33]

It is this going forth of the inner light in the form of its
rays, like a child leaving its mother and its home to "explore"
the world without finding what it looks for—a place where it
can feel "at home"—and its return to its source, the child
going back to its mother and its (legitimate) dwelling; that is,
the theme of the stories of the present study. It also has been
the theme of a beautiful allegory—"the symbols through
which the mystery of Being expresses itself"—which Padmasambhava lets the *ḍākinīs*, female personifications of the
fundamental forces in their luminous aspects experienced
within us as *anima*-like figures, tell:[34]

In a temple[35] (made of) a luminosity (that is) the purity
(of its symbolicalness) and the glare of the phenomenal,[36] archetypal Man (*khye'u chung*), all-knowing and
lord of phantoms,[37] "Genuine-Strength" by name and
goddess "Blazing Light," the beautiful *lumen naturale*
(as which Being's) predisposition to become alight (has
become an actual light), became husband and wife and
through their intimate union as Father (*yab*) and Mother
(*yum*) a son, the "self-begotten *lumen naturale* (as
being) all-sensitive"[38] was conceived in the Mother. The
son went to look for the limits of space by travelling
over the eight cardinal points, but he did not find either
the limits or the center. Having rid himself of his concepts and propositions about the world in its phenomenal presence and interpretation as samsara and nirvana—
this is the innermost instruction about submerging into
the vortex of the whole's energy—he did not find any
place to go further and so returned (home). Out of fear
that he might be abducted by terrifying enemies he did
not travel again but, holding in his hands the Wish-

granting Jewel, he stayed at home. Without there being any necessity on his part to toil laboriously in order to achieve anything, whatever he wished for came about spontaneously. He could dismiss the thought of still having something to do and could feel like a person who has finished his work. Without having to look for something to do and then laboriously to accomplish it, (whatever constituted his) reality was a *fait accompli*. Through understanding his reality that existed since time before time all expectations and apprehensions were eradicated—this is (indicated by the term) *thig-le nyag-gcig*,[39] the symbol through which the mystery of Being expresses itself.

In this passage the impact of non-Indian ideas on the formation of early rDzogs-chen thought is explicitly stated. This is the intriguing image of "archetypal Man" as which I render the technical term *khye'u chung*.[40] Wherever this image occurs it is associated with light, be this the *lumen naturale* or, most frequently, its auto-presencing in an auto-dynamic lighting-up. Archetypal Man is further characterized as a self-sufficient cognitively ecstatic intensity[41] and as one in whom the whole's and, by implication, the individual human being's predisposition to becoming individuated is alight.[42] In the symbolic language, so much favored by the early rDzogs-chen thinkers, this intensity is of the transparency of a crystal—"crystal archetypal Man,"[43] or of the freshness of youth—"youthful archetypal Man,"[44] who conducts a dialogue with the teacher "Utterly-free-of-boundaries."[45] Whether Padmasambhava borrowed and adapted the idea of archetypal Man from the Gnostic idea of the "Adam of Light"[46]—Adam being the prototype of humankind—cannot be stated with certainly, but he certainly seems to have been well acquainted with the light symbolism of the Manichaeans who at about his time flourished in Turkestan where they had spread from Eastern Iran. "Demythologizing" the relationship between the "archetypal Man" and the teacher "Utterly-free-of-boundaries," we can say that for Padmasambhava archetypal Man is the excitation of a field that has no boundary but nevertheless prompts its excitation that thus is the larval stage of the individuation process. The complexity of this evolutionary image has been described by Padmasambhava as follows:[47]

> In a house (made of) the luminosity of (Being's expanse as a) field of (possible meanings) and the glare of the phenomenal[48]
> Man's fore-structure,[49] the depth and vastness of (the whole's) primal-beginning-that-is-not, and
> (His/its) predisposition to become alight radiating since its originary presencing, self-originated, and
> (He himself as) Archetypal Man (alight) by himself in the light (of being the *lumen naturale*) and in the purity (of being Being's symbolicalness)[50]
> Has to be encountered in such a manner that none (of these three facets) can be added to or subtracted from the other.

In other words, archetypal Man is, in modern terms, a *process-structure*, whose "structure" is already prefigured (not predetermined) in what we cannot but refer to as the "ground-that-is-not"[51] and whose "process," its unfolding, is in its primal-beginning-that-is-not,[52] resulting in the manifest form that had latently been present. As such a process-structure, archetypal Man is not weighted down by considerations of sex with which ancient Greek, Gnostic and Judaeo-Christian thinking was preoccupied,[53] a preoccupation that in modern times lingers on unabatedly in Freudian psychology.

This brief survey of the salient ideas of early[54] rDzogs-chen thought hints at the likely locale in which they originated. Their systematization as well as their further development in the course of their systematization goes back to the "instructor" or "great instructor"[55] Padmasambhava, hailing from the same country as his predecessor dGa'-rab rdo-rje,[56] a native from Dhanakośa (as yet unidentified, but probably an important trading center on the Silk Route[57]) in Uḍḍiyāna

(Urgyan),[58] who is claimed to have been the humanly concrete "originator" of this line of thought. Although we may speak of the "great instructor" Padmasambhava—Guru Rinpoche as he is respectfully and endearingly called by the Tibetans—as a systematizer, this must not allow us to overlook or become forgetful of the fact that he was an independent thinker whose thinking was suffused by the acknowledged experience of the *lumen naturale*. His written works certainly reflect the then prevailing *Zeitgeist*, a lively interest in cosmogonies and anthropogonies, the former determined by a dualistic view and the latter by a tripartite scissure. His process-oriented thinking at once distances him from any dualistic and static-monistic forms of thought. It also distances him from the Gnostics who, because of the low esteem in which they held the world and the human individual, were forced to develop a soteriology that in one form or another became normative of Western religious thinking. By him as well as other rDzogs-chen thinkers, these same themes of cosmogony and anthropogony were viewed from the perspective of wholeness: the whole evolves through a series of symmetry breaks into an interplay of macroevolutionary and microevolutionary forces that at every level of their organization are capable of a linking backward to the origin as an opening of new developing lines. The linking backward process is not so much a circular motion in the strict sense of the word, rather it is a kind of a spiral movement that the experiencer who is this movement, may "sense" as his/her going up (ascent) or going down (descent)— an "upward unfolding and/or downward going astray."[59]

Leaving aside their individualistic implications in the Western context ascent and descent are two of the few process words and concepts in the predominantly static world view that the West inherited from the post-Heraclitan Greek tradition which became reinforced and rigidified by Aristotelian categories that greatly hampered a person's gaining insight into the dynamics of experience. These process words graphically and vividly illustrate any living individual's tortuous journey through life. This journey with all its

ups and downs may be watched in a more or less dispassion-
ate and detached manner as going on "out there" on the
physical plane,[60] but it may also be felt to go on "in here,"
deep within ourselves on the psychological and spiritual levels, and is then described in images such as lifting a shining
jewel out of the mud into which it had slipped or as unlock-
ing the door behind which the treasure of life's deepest mystery is lying.

Actually, this mystery underlies all aspects of our sociocultural life—a person's sociality overtly expressing itself in
his always being-with-others and culture being the expression of shared values that vary according to the level in the
individual's hierarchical organization on which they are
operative. These shared values are suffused with mythological and, by implication, psychological connotations[61] that
only too often become debased by religious and other ideologically prescriptive preferences raised to inviolate postulates and dogmas of absoluteness that by locking up the
individual's simultaneously sensual-sensuous and intuitive-
spiritual mode of knowing cannot but stifle all life. It
becomes therefore all the more necessary to unlock the door
that bars a person from living a life worth living. As Padmasambhava said:

> By opening the iron lock on the door (behind which
>   Being's) mystery (lies)
> You will come across the treasure of your existential
>   reality (that is Being's) energy.[62]

There are many doors of a sociocultural nature, ritualistic
and ideological, that have to be opened.[63] Padmasambhava's
integrity as a thinker[64]—some might say, his radicalism—
shows itself in the fact that he does not exempt his own systems[65] from the verdict of being a door that has to be
unlocked:[66]

> By opening the door (called) "verbiage-mongering
>   about Being"

With the key (called) "glare of the phenomenal
    dissipating into nothing"
You will see (Being's) nonexistent birth [in its] pure and
    primal symbolicalness [that is the] fore-structure [of
    your individuation].[67]

Opening the doors of the various prisons we have built for
ourselves does not only make us come across the treasure and
mystery of our life, it also opens and broadens our vision by
unmasking the absurdity of our mind's hard-to-overcome
structure-orientation—there must be a recognized and
already preexisting goal or end-state. Let us get rid of the prevailing reductionism that conceives of seeing as a passive
receptivity and bear in mind that seeing is always interpretation. Seeing the fore-structure of one's individuation is
already an interpretation of this structure as being meaning.
But how does interpretation enter the picture? Certainly not
from outside. Let us bear in mind that wholeness—the Being-
that-is-not in Padmasambhava's words—is not the same as a
totality. The latter can be summed up by the parts that make
up a totality as an objective closure; the former cannot.[68] It is
a single indivisible and irreducible reality whose "oneness" or
"uniqueness"[69] may be likened to a single quantum state that
in its not being a thing[70] (whether material or immaterial) is
an "openness"—a (dynamic) "nothingness" that is neither
some void nor *some* emptiness but, if any predication is per-
missible, the fullness or nothingness of pure intensity.[71]
Because of its being pure intensity it is for ever active in the
manner of the quantum state's quantum wave functions
(replete with possibilities and probabilities) in letting intensities pass as subintensities of itself. These, then, occupy some
space-like space to the degree of the intensity in its subinten-
sity and in this autospatialization set up a timelike time as the
speed with which the spatialization occurs. In so doing,
wholeness creates its own boundary conditions[72] for its own
activity. We may conceive of this pure intensity as intense
matter, unformed yet allowing patterns to form as intense

magnitudes. These magnitudinal patterns are the gestalts into which wholeness molds itself so that it would be more correct to speak of them (in the plural) as *Gestaltungen*, rather than (in the singular) as a gestalt. Because of the centrality of the human body in experience these magnitudinal patterns or gestalt/*Gestaltungen* are assessed in terms of the experiencer's body as the whole's "body"-gestalt,[73] a gestalt that has as yet no face nor hands[74] and, as such, only prefigures the whole's passage into the dimension of humanness. This is what Padmasambhava understands by "Being" and "Being's lighting-up (or coming-to-presence)."[75]

In this lighting-up as the whole's auto-presencing, Being's (the whole's) dynamics is "felt" as energy whose luminosity as its creativity is quite literally "seen" in and as multicolored rays of light. Their iridescence can thus be said to be the sensuously visible aspect of the otherwise invisible energy (that is Being in its sheer intensity) and of the otherwise invisible light already in this intensity. But there is more to these rays of light than their visibility. They have "something to say"[76] to those who are exceptional in their capacity to hear.[77] In the *Rig-pa rang-shar*,[78] we are told in a terse, imaginatively rich statement that: "(Being) having entered (and become) the light of its gestalt frolics in the rays of its speech."

In this pronouncement, we can, in terms of modern science easily recognize the interdependence of structure and function; its deeper meaning, however, is that the supraconscious ecstatic intensity that is Being, molds itself into a gestalt as the fore-structure of Being's individuation process that in itself is Being's *lumen naturale*. This gestalt communicates with its environing field, it "speaks" and in so doing "has something to say" (which is not the same as the noise pollution of talking, euphemistically called "delivering a speech"), and what is communicated is the *lumen naturale* by way of the latter's rays.

In the same vein as Padmasambhava had spoken of Being and its lighting up or coming-to-presence, he now speaks of (Being's) "energy" and its "creativity-as-rays-of-light":[79]

Wherever sun and moon exist they radiate their light,
Wherever (Being's) energy extends its creativity comes-
to-light in rays of light

When we say that the world is full of colors, we tacitly admit
that the things we see, each in its own way, shine in their own
light but then, in order not to be lumped together with those
whose vision is exceptional, we revert to the widely accepted
"unseeing" mode of seeing and deal with what we see in terms
of drab substances only accidentally modified by qualities.
This means that we have closed ourselves to the light that is
Being and from the perspective of this closure now interpret
what lights up as our phenomenal world by a categorical
scheme that reflects the narrowness of rational, representational thinking whose mainstay is logic. Paradoxically, rational
thought is only a more glaring and hence blinding manifestation of something larger that is already presupposed by it, but
for obvious reasons dismissed as of little or no importance. We
may content ourselves with saying, as the Buddhists did, that
the world is our thoughts; what we actually want is to come to
grips with the *thinking* of thinking, to which we point by such
words as "mind," often spelled with a capital letter *M* to distinguish it from the petty ego-logical "consciousness" (loosely
called "mind"), and/or "spirit/spirituality," all of them, in one
way or another, unsatisfactory because of their predominantly
static connotations.[80] It is thinking that as the *thinking* of
thinking, like the light that we are, constitutes us as being both
beings and humans. The less we think the less we are and the
less we are human. Again it is Padmasambhava who draws our
attention to our being thinking (rational-emotional) beings by
using the key terms of Buddhist logic and infusing them with
new life. He speaks of the multiplicity of our phenomenal
world that is always an interpreted world,[81] a probability distribution, as logical constructs.[82] Primarily these logical constructs, that is, before they are turned into constructs in the
strict sense of the word, are playful self-manifestation of the
internal logic of Being,[83] as Padmasambhava tells us:[84]

In (Being's) pre- and proto-initial thereness[85] for which
there is no name (and which as Being's) internal logic
(is Being's) non-origin,
All that originates by itself (out of Being's non-origin
and thus is Being's) own creativity (and in) branching
out (comes as Being's) play
(Turns out to be Being's) errancy into mistaken
identifications (prompted) by the disruptive intellect
and must be indicted as such.

He then goes on to tell us that Being's internal logic is
Being itself and what is called its errancy into mistaken identifications, that which makes up our phenomenal world, is
our intellect's failure to comprehend and understand[86] the
creative dynamics in Being's energy.

In Being's internal logic [Being's possibilizing
dynamics] that is Being itself there does not exist any
errancy into mistaken identifications:
Just as in a crystal mirror whatever is placed before it—
Be this something white or red or some medicine or
poison—will appear (in it and make the mirror seem
to be what is placed before it),
So in the energy that is Being (displaying an) origin-
that-is-not
The rays (that are its) creativity may appear (originate)
as so many mistaken identifications
They are not intrinsic to Being that remains as pure as it
has been.[87]

The mistaken identifications of whose origin Padmasambhava speaks in this stanza are what elsewhere he had termed
"logical constructs" and what he wants to imply by speaking
of mistaken identifications is that we should not be carried
away by this errancy mode of thought. The reason is that the
more intense our failure to comprehend and to understand
grows and the more we depend on the logical constructs that

make up our world and in whose absolute validity we believe only because we have constructed them, the more the light that we are and by which we see and which "speaks" *of* (not *about*) the wealth of our existential reality grows dimmer and dimmer so that, in the end, we begin to feel like having been cast into a prison whose darkness hides from our view the treasure that is ours. In metaphorical language—actually all language is metaphorical—this being cast into a prison is spoken of as an individual's descent or abduction, which in the two individuation stories here presented serves as a preamble to the hero and heroine's adventures in ascending to and regaining their wholeness. In the first story, the problem which all mankind faces is how to get out of the prison and move again into the light from which we unwittingly allowed ourselves to be taken away. In the second story the problem is to retrieve the light that we are, but that somehow we allowed it to be swallowed up by darkness. In either case, the solution, if we may say so, lies in reversing the trend to go "down" and astray into the lightless mistaken identifications by understanding and in this understanding moving "up." This is a task each of us must perform alone. There may be helpers but they cannot do the job for us. Unlike in Gnosticism with which Padmasambhava was acquainted and which to a certain extent may have influenced his thinking, there is in all rDzogs-chen thinkers' process-oriented thinking no god who descends to earth to redeem humankind. Humankind redeems itself by itself and that is what the individuation process is about.

Notes

1. They form the thirty-ninth and fortieth chapter, respectively, of the *Rig-pa rang-shar*, pp. 561–578. This huge work received its final form at the time of the Tibetan king Khri-srong lde-brtsan (b. 740/742). The two chapters have been incorporated with additional glosses in Klong-chen rab-'byams-pa's *Theg-pa'i mchog rin-po-che'i mdzod* [abbr.: *Theg-mchog*] (vol. 1, pp. 324–330). A slightly more "polished" version is found in the second volume, pp. 605–630, of the *rDzogs-pa-chen-po dgongs-pa zang-thal*, a huge collection of texts "rediscovered from their places of

concealment at Zang-zang Lha-brag" in 1366/67 by rGod-kyi ldem-'phru-can (1327–1386).

2. Plato's indebtedness to Pythagoras is well attested to in the *Timaeus*, an unfinished, largely theoretical work. In this work, he takes up the Pythagorean distinction between the Limited (*peras*) and the Unlimited (*apeiron*) whose harmonious mixture according to Pythagoras gives rise to the phenomenal universe. But then Plato goes on to speak of the *peras* as the One and of the *apeiron* as the indeterminate dyad, which he splits up into the masculine *logos* and the feminine *eros*. On the basis of his irrational belief in male superiority, he identifies the masculine *logos* with "good" and the feminine *eros* with "evil." This bias was to have devastating consequences for the ethico-religious and sociocultural life of the Western world, as discussed at length by Nel Noddings, *Women and Evil*. For details of the Pythagorean-Platonic connection see David R. Fidler's *Introduction* to Kenneth Sylvan Guthrie, *The Pythagorean Sourcebook and Library*.

3. The relationship between Neoplatonism, whose leading proponent, Plotinus, attempts to overcome Plato's dualism with his notion of the One (standing above the Monad and the Dyad), and the Gnostic dualism(s) is extremely antagonistic. In his *Enneads*, he repeatedly attacks the Gnostics because of their negative evaluation of the cosmos and its creator. Nonetheless, he must admit, though grudgingly, that they strive for a higher world with an otherworldly and unknown God. An excellent discussion of this antagonism between Platonic and gnostic forms of dualism is found in Kurt Rudolph, *Gnosis*, pp. 59ff.

4. On the distinction between structure orientation and process orientation see Erich Jantsch, *Design for Evolution*, p. 24 and passim.

5. See Kenneth Sylvan Guthrie, *Pythagorean Sourcebook*, p. 40.

6. VI, 9,3.

7. This version is taken from *Plotinus: The Enneads*, translated by Stephen MacKenna, p. 539. In *The Essential Plotinus*, edited by Elmer O'Brien, this passage reads:

As the One begets all things, it cannot be any of them—
neither thing, nor quality, nor quantity, nor intelligence, nor soul.

Plotinus attempts to overcome Plato's rigid dualism by introducing the idea of serial emanations: the first emanation is *nous* (mind or intelligence), the second is *psyche* (soul).

8. The *Byang-chub-sems-kyi man-ngag rin-chen phreng-ba* (sDe-dge ed. vol. 6, fol. 161a) explicitly conceives of it as a linguistic device to rid ourselves of certain preconceptions:

In order to get rid of the notion of existence I speak of non-existence; (in order to get rid of the notion of there being) a middle I speak of non-duality; in order to get rid of the notion of non-duality I speak of oneness (*nyag-gcig*); in order to get rid of the notion of oneness I speak of non-conceptualization; in order to get rid of the notion of non-conceptualization I speak of ineffability; and in order to get rid of the notion of ineffability I speak of an opening (*kha-'phyam*).

The rendering of the term *kha-'phyam* is tentative. It is not found in any dictionary. It is used in connection with an unobstructed vision and "explained" by a subsequent verse to the effect that it is

Like brandishing a spear in the air—
Wherever one aims it it will not hit anything.

9. The term autopoietic is derived from the term "autopoiesis" that was coined by the Chilean biologist Francisco Varela and further developed together with Humberto Maturana and Ricardo Uribe. As explicated by Erich Jantsch, *The Self-organizing Universe*, p. 7: "Autopoiesis refers to the characteristic of living systems to continuously renew themselves and to regulate this process in such a way that the integrity of their structure is maintained."

10. This text is ascribed to 'Jam-dpal bshes-gnyen and preserved in the *rGyud-'bum* of Vairocana, vol. 7, pp. 287–340. The passage quoted is found on p. 293.

11. In this triad of *yul*, *sems*, and *bdag*, the term *bdag* "self/Self" is one of the most difficult ones. What is meant by it in rDzogs-chen thought and its distillation, the sNying-thig literature, is the experiencer's existential reality, termed *don* by Padmasambhava in his *rGyud thams-cad-kyi rgyal-po Nyi-zla'i snying-po 'od-'bar-ba bdud-rtsi rgya-mtsho 'khyil-ba'i rgyud* [abbr.: *Nyi-zla'i snying-po*] (sDe-dge ed., vol. 3, fols. 18b–46b), fols. 19b, 10b, 28b, and by Klong-chen rab-'byams-pa in his *Zab-mo yang-tig* [abbr.: *Zab-yang*] I, p. 299. Since this reality is cognitive through and through, it is termed "*rig-pa*" in his *gNas-lugs rin-po-che'i mdzod*], p. 75. From the perspective of wholeness *rig-pa* is its "supraconscious ecstatic intensity." In order to become "conscious of itself," this unpolarized energy polarizes itself into what we call "consciousness" or "(subjective) mind" (*sems*) and its cognitive domain, the "object" (*yul*). In other words, one, in becoming two, becomes three simultaneously. This is what is meant by the "autocatalysis of consciousness," a phrase coined by Erich Jantsch, *Design for Evolution*, p. 107—for want of an appropriate term for this "third" force.

12. The full title is *Ye-shes gsang-ba sgron-me rin-po-che man-ngag-gi rgyud*. It is found in volume 6, fols. 248b–257a of the sDe-dge edition of the *rNying-ma rgyud-'bum*. The only commentary on it, probably by Vairocana himself, the *rDzogs-chen gsang-ba'i sgron-me'i rgyud 'grel chen-mo*, is preserved in the *rGyud-'bum* of Vairocana, vol. 7, pp. 111–247, though in a garbled form. The thirteenth chapter of Śrīsiṃha's work deals with the idea of the *kun-gzhi* "one's ontical foundation." For details see my *From Reductionism to Creativity: rDzogs-chen and the New Sciences of Mind*, pp. 212ff. The above quoted passage is on fol. 255b.

13. *rang-sems*. The term *rang* "self" is in this compound used reflexively. Since we do not *have* something called "mind" but *are* mind, I have rendered this term by "(one's) self-reflexive mind."

14. *mnyam-pa-nyid*. Literally rendered this term corresponds to our notion of "homogeneity"; technically speaking it intimates what we would call the "principle of self-consistency." For its definition see Erich Jantsch, *The Self-organizing Universe*, p.32.

15. In all editions available to me, the line that should begin with *nyag* is missing. However, in his aforementioned commentary, p. 226, Vairocana states: " *nyag* means (the whole's) supraconscious ecstatic intensity that cannot be comprehended intellectually. The supraconscious ecstatic intensity is dissociated from anything that allows itself to be concretized."

16. The full title is *sPros-bral don-gsal chen-po'i rgyud* (sDe-dge ed., vol. 1, fols. 1–89b), fol. 7a. This work, which is a systematic presentation of rDzogs-chen thought, has been largely forgotten. Its abbreviated version, the *Thig-le kun-gsal man-ngag-gi bshad-rgyud* (sDe-dge ed., vol. 4, fols. 213a–278b), is frequently quoted by Klong-chen rab-'byams-pa.

17. This interpretation of the compound *snang-srid* goes back to Padmasambhava's *sNang-srid kha-sbyor bdud-rtsi bcud-thigs 'khor-ba thog-mtha' gcod-pa'i rgyud* [abbr.: *sNang-srid kha-sbyor*] (sDe-dge ed. vol. 2, fols. 204a–265b), fol. 235a:

snang-ba means the external objective cognitive domain,
srid-pa means means the internal subjective mind,
kha-sbyor means that (the above two) do not form a duality.

The text continues giving further examples and concludes the enumeration with the significant statement that

snang-ba means the perishable world (as a container),
srid-pa means the totality of sentient beings (in it),
kha-sbyor means that (evaluations such as) good and bad and
(judgments such as) negation and affirmation are inapplicable.

The version of this lengthy work in the Thimpu edition of the *rNying-ma rgyud-'bum* (vols. 5, pp. 526–601 and vol. 6, pp. 2–52) differs in some respects considerably from the one in the sDe-dge edition.

This text is one of five auxiliary texts to the *sPros-bral don-gsal* that deal with the "cutting off" (*gcod-pa*) of the conceptual-propositional impediments (*spros-pa*) that prevent our existential reality (*don*) from shining in all its brightness (*gsal*). The four remaining ones are the *Rin-po-che bcud-kyi yang-snying thog-ma'i dras-thag gcod-pa spros-pa gcod-pa rtsa-ba'i rgyud* [abbr.: *sPros-pa gcod-pa rtsa-ba*] (sDe-ge ed., vol. 2, fols. 266a–271b), the *sPros-pa gcod-pa sde-lnga'i rgyud* [abbr.: *sPros-pa gcod-pa sde-nga*] (ibid., fols. 271b-277a), the *Rin-po-che bdud-rtsi bcud-thigs-kyi rgyud* [abbr.: *bDud-rtsi bcud-thigs*] (ibid., fols. 277b–287a), and the *Rin-po-che snang-gsal spu-gri 'bar-bas 'khrul-snang rtsad-nas gcod-pa nam-mkha'i mtha' dang mnyam-pa'i rgyud* [abbr: *Nam-mkha'i mtha' dang mnyam-pa*.

18. *gzhi-med*. The Tibetan language is very precise in distinguishing between an "is not" (*min*) as describing something existing as not having this or that property, and an "is not" (*med*) as denying (something's) existence.

19. *Nam-mkha'i mtha' dang mnyam-pa*, fol. 288b.

20. *gnas-pa'i gzhi*. I have chosen the Heideggerian term "Dasein" for the Tibetan *gnas/gnas-pa*, as it comes closest, when read as *Da*-sein (with the emphasis on the *Da* "there") to what is understood by it in rDzogs-chen thought.

21. For the benefit of the reader, I have inserted this line on the basis of Padmasambhava's lengthy elaboration of this stanza, its first topic being the irreducibility of the whole (the lake) to either this or that—the "is not" (*min*), as pointed out in note 18.

22. This line implies the "is not" (*med*), as pointed out in note 18. There is a subtle progression from the "smaller" to the "larger" that psychologically means that the "irrealization" (a term coined by C. G. Jung) of our ordinary world becomes intensified.

23. *mnyam-pa-nyid*. See also note 14.

24. *dngos-po gshis-kyi gnas-lugs*; *Nam-mkha'i mtha' dang mnyam-pa*, fol. 289a. This term may be tentatively translated as "the presence of Being (in and as) the concrete." It is found only in works of an experiential character.

25. Buddhist thinkers never made the preposterous statement that the world *is* an illusion; it may be *like* an illusion (*sgyu-ma lta-bu*, Skt. *māyopama*), and between the *is* and the *like* there is a tremendous difference.

26. *khyab-pa'i gzhi; Nam-mkha'i mtha' dang mnyam-pa*, fol. 289a.

27. *g.yo-ba'i gzhi; Nam-mkha'i mtha' dang mnyam-pa*, fol. 289a.

28. The variety of terms referring to a "time-before-time" in the Tibetan language is unparalleled in any Western language. There are three terms: *sngon, thog- (ma)*, and *ye*. Of these the two terms "pre-initial" (*sngon*) and "proto-initial" (*thog*) are frequently used in their combination of *sngon-thog*, implying a kind of continuity of a "beginning-before-a-beginning," a "time-before-time." Of special importance is the use of this compound with the term *spyi-phud* "the primal nothing that harbors in itself the idea of (what becomes our) world," anthropomorphically imaged as "teacher" (*ston-pa*) whose name is "energy (as) the beingness of Being (*snying-po de-kho-na-nyid*)." See *Nyi-zla'i snying-po*, fol. 18b–19a: *sngon-thog spyi-phud-kyi ston-pa snying-po de-kho-na-nyid*. Equally intriguing is the use of this compound with the term *dmag-dpon* "army commander"; on fol. 32a, which seems to show Padmasambhava's familiarity with the Gnostic idea of "archons." Unfortunately the phrase *snying-po klong-yangs chos-nyid dkyil-'khor-na / sngon-thog spyi-phud lha-chen ka-dag bzhugs* (on fol. 37a) is difficult to interpret. The word *lha-chen* can be interpreted as the "unknown God" of Basilides or as Śiva Mahādeva. The other highly technical terms like *snying-po, klong-yangs*, and *ka-dag* are rDzogs-chen terms that will be discussed later on. As further evidence for Padmasambhava's familiarity with the ideas of the Gnostics, in particular with the ideas of Basilides, I refer to his use of the term *spyi-mes* "Fore-father" in the sentence *snang-srid thams-cad-kyi spyi-mes sngon-thog khri-rje* (on fols. 28b–29a) "the Fore-father of the whole phenomenal world, the *sngon-thog* myriarch named gTsug-brtan grags-pa*," where "myriarch" is obviously Padmasambhava's (?) rendering of the Gnostic idea of the archon whose "description" is in part reproduced at the end of the second story in the present study.

29. *rlung*. In modern terminology we would speak of an "inner dynamics" experienced to move like a breeze or a kind of turbulence.

30. *'byung-ba'i gzhi; Nam-mkha'i mtha' dang mnyam-pa*, fol. 289a.

31. See for instance the *sPros-pa gcod-pa rtsa-ba*, fol. 268a. The Tibetan term I have rendered by "energy" is *snying-po*. It is etymologically related to *snying-ga* "heart." The implication is that "energy" as understood by Padmasambhava is primarily "psychic/spiritual," not physical. As is well known, C. G. Jung, too, spoke of "psychic energy" and, with this term, he distanced himself from Freud's reductionism.

32. *Nam-mkha'i mtha' dang mnyam-pa*, fol. 309b. Similar, but slightly more expanded, is the presentation of this process on fol. 289 of the same work, where the term *'od* "light" is used instead of *snying-po*.

33. Non-origination, a birth-that-is-not (*skye-med*) and invariance, a change-that-is-not (*'gyur-med*) are ontological terms, not quality words or adjectives accidentally modifying some object or subject, depending on whether one subscribes to the myth of objectivism or the myth of subjectivism. This insistence on non-existence (*med*) of which we have to think and of which we attempt to speak in words that act more as prison bars than openings, has been and still is a stumbling block for us who cannot but think in terms of things, as it has been for the Indian Buddhists. The story goes that Asanga, who was more of a propagator of Yogācāra ideas rather than an original thinker, had to return to his teacher Maitreya (whoever this person may have been) for clarification of the idea of non-existence (*abhūta*) presented in his, that is, Maitreya's *Uttaratantraśāstra*. Does this not point to some non-Indian origin? Certainly, the Madhyama system's negativistic reductionism run amok completely fails to awaken in the listener a heightened, supraconscious ecstatic intensity that is at the very heart of rDzogs-chen teaching, cryptically intimated by the "taking up one's legitimate dwelling."

34. *Nyi-zla'i snying-po*, fol. 33a.

35. *lha-khang*. The use of this term immediately calls to mind the Gnostic idea of the "Bridal Chamber," which is the "Holy of Holies." For details see Kurt Rudolph, *Gnosis*, pp. 245f.

36. This phrase, *snang-gsal rnam-dag 'od-kyi lha-khang-na*, occurs at the beginning of the chapter from which the above account is taken as *rin-chen snang-gsal 'od-gsal-gyi lha-khang-na* and on fol. 43b as *snang-gsal chos-dbyings-'od khang-du*. On fols. 24b and 37b the two light intensities, *snang-gsal* and *'od-gsal*, are illustrated by the sun (*nyi-ma*) and the moon (*zla-ba*) respectively. In these phrases, the adjective *rnam-dag* "pure (as to observable qualities)" and the noun *chos-dbyings* "Being's field-like expanse as the matrix of meanings" have been used interchangeably. The symbols of sun and moon are used by Rong-zom Chos-kyi bzang-po (tenth century) in his *gSang-'grel*, fol. 44b, to illustrate the principle of complementarity as commonly expressed by "operacy," the whole's effectiveness principle (*thabs*, Skt. *upāya*) and "appreciation," the whole's auto-intensification of its cognitive-appreciative capacity (*shes-rab*, Skt. *prajñā*), describing an organism's functional properties.

37. *'phrul-gyi rje*. This may well be an allusion to the Nirmāṇarati and Paranirmitavaśavartin gods in Indian Buddhist cosmology. See Vasubandhu's *Abhidharmakośa* III 69b–d. They still belong to the world of sensuality (Kāmadhātu) and their sex life consists of smiling and looking at each other, respectively. Here the Buddhist idea of having intercourse without a sexual union tallies with the Gnostic idea of the bridal

chamber as a sacrament that only at some later stage involved a sexual act. See Kurt Rudolph, *Gnosis*, pp. 245ff. 256, and Benjamin Walker, *Gnosticism*, pp. 123f.

38. Attention should be drawn to the difference in the qualification of archetypal Man as "all-knowing" (*kun-rig*) and of the son as "all-sensitive" (*kun-mkhyen*). *kun-rig* is used ontologically—archetypal Man is supraconscious ecstatic intensity through and through; *kun-mkhyen* is used epistemologically—the son still has to learn how to grow into the ecstatic intensity.

39. For a tentative rendering of this term see note 9.

40. Literally translated this term means a "little child" under ten years of age that may be a boy (*pho*) or a girl (*mo*), but in the present context is certainly understood as being a "boy." This is about all it has in common with the "child archetype," the *puer aeternus*, in Western thought, of which C. G. Jung has made a special study in his *The Archetypes and the Collective Unconscious*, pp. 151ff. More intriguing is the emphasis on its holistic luminosity (*ngang-dangs*) and smallness (*chung*)—the word *khye'u* itself is already a diminutive—which, superficially looked at, reminds us of the idea of the *homunculus* who since antiquity and, specifically, in medieval alchemical literature, was an articificially produced diminutive man of magical power (see, for instance, C. G. Jung, *Psychology and Alchemy*, *Alchemical Studies*, s.v., and Johannes Fabricius, *Alchemy*, s.v.). However, there is nothing artificial about the *khye'u chung*. Rather, as archetypal Man, a powerful symbol of wholeness, he is more akin to the Gnostic idea of the Anthropos, "a unitary being who existed before man and at the same time represents man's goal" (C. G. Jung, *Psychology and Alchemy*, p. 162); and the idea of the *photeinos anthropos* (*Lichtmensch*, Man of Light), occurring in Sufism (see Henry Corbin, *Avicenna and the Visionary Recital*, pp. 231f.). In this connection it may not be out of place to refer to Johann Wolfgang von Goethe's differentiation between what is natural and what is artificial:

Das ist die Eigenschaft der Dinge:
Natürlichem genügt das Weltall kaum,
Was künstlich ist, verlangt geschlossnen Raum
Such is the property of things:
To what is natural the universe can hardly offer space enough,
While what is artificial demands closed space.

(*Faust*, "Laboratory," part II, vs. 6882–6884)

Specifically, the similarity of the *khye'u chung* idea with the notion of the docetists about the heavenly Christ cannot be disputed. As Kurt

Rudolph, *Gnosis*, p. 167 points out, according to them "the heavenly Christ, who possessed the fullness of the aeons, only came down upon earth by stripping himself of all glory, and making himself quite small, like 'a lightning flash in a minute body.'" A further similarity is found in the fact that while in the Gnostic account the heavenly Christ in his descent is "accompanied" by an Angel, in the Buddhist story the *khye'u chung* in his descent into the "world", as detailed in our second story, is "accompanied" by five servants as behoves his exalted status.

41. *rang-rig*. This technical term is an ontological concept, not an epistemological concept as it has been misunderstood by Buddhist philosophers, notably Nagarjuna. In order to be known what is meant by it, it must be experienced by oneself.

42. *ngang-dangs*, sometimes also spelled *ngang-dvangs*, is a process-product word that is frequently met with in works by Padmasambhava. See for instance his *sNang-srid kha-sbyor*, fol. 208b. Here it is used with reference to the "greatness" (*che-ba*) of the process structure (*sangs-rgyas*) rendered by "Buddha" (as if it referred to the *thing*-person described as "having become spiritually awake," a description turned into a proper name). Padmasambhava's words are:

Once dichotomic thought has gone (*sangs*) originary awareness has
    unfolded (*rgyas*);
It is not the case that someone has placed (something) into
    (something called the) unfolded —
(Wholeness) itself (*rang-nyid*) has unfolded by itself (*rang-gis*).

43. *shel-gyi khye'u chung*. See *Thig-le gsang-ba'i brda'i rgyud* (sDe-dge ed., vol. 25, fols. (49b-53b), fols. 51b. On fol. 52a the short form *shel-gyi khye'u* is given.

44. *khye'u chung gzhon-nu*; fol. 52a, p. 487.

45. *mu-mtha' yongs-grol*. Padmasambhava's work opens with the statement:

In the endlessly upward and downward spiralling vortex (*kha-gting med-pa'i klong*) of Being's possibilizing dynamics the teacher Self-existent Boundary-free (*rang-byung mu-mtha' [yongs]-grol*) explained his radiance-*cum*-purity self-emancipation (*gsal-dag rang-grol*) teaching to the assembly of an auto-presencing light (*rang-snang 'od*). At this regal time that had neither a beginning nor end (*thog-mtha' med-pa'i dus*) the recorder (of the teaching) was archetypal Man, a self-sufficient cognitively ecstatic intensity (*rang-rig khye'u chung*).

46. Mentioned in the Nag Hammadi Codex II, tractate 5. See James M. Robinson, ed., *The Nag Hammadi Library in English*, pp. 170–189, and also Kurt Rudolph, *Gnosis*, pp. 75f., 95ff.

47. *Nyi-zla'i snying-po*, fol. 43b.

48. On this symbolism of light see also note 36.

49. The technical term *chos-sku* is inexhaustible in meanings and hence defies any reductionist definition. Wherever and whenever it is used in the original texts it has "symbolic pregance." This phrase was coined and defined by Ernst Cassirer, *Philosophie der symbolischen Formen*, vol. 3, p. 235, vol. 3, p. 202 in the English translation *The Philosophy of Symbolic Forms*. Combining both the orginal German version and the English translation, John Michael Krois, *Cassirer: Symbolic Forms and History*, p. 54, states: "By symbolic pregnance we mean the way [*die Art*] in which a perception as a 'sensory' experience ['*sinnliches' Erlebnis*] contains at the same time a certain nonintuitive 'meaning' ['*Sinn*'] which it immediately and concretely represents."

50. *rang-gsal dag-pa*. The term *rang-gsal* means that archetypal Man shines in humankind's own (*rang*) light or *lumen naturale* (*'od-gsal*), not in some borrowed light; *dag-pa* points to Being's (the whole's) primal symbolicalness (*ka-dag*) that makes any symbolic pregnance possible. On "symbolic pregnance" see preceding note. The technical term *dag-pa* is basically descriptive of an experience of a supraordinate clarity in what is the whole's primal (*ka*) "purity" or symbolicalness (*dag*) as yet untainted by the "impurity" or opacity (*ma-dag-pa*) of representational constructs (*rnam-pa*) with which the mind (*sems*) as a low-level intensity (*ma-rig-pa*) of the whole's supraconscious ecstatic intensity busies itself.

51. See for instancce *Nyi-zla'i snying-po*, fol. 21b:
gzhi-med ngang-las kun gzhi shar
Out of the (evolutionary) disposition of the ground-that-is-not the ground for all (that is) has arisen.

52. *ye-med*.

53. Androgyny is a static concept that plays a prominent role in structure-oriented thought as exemplified by the thought forms just mentioned. See Benjamin Walker, *Gnosticism*, pp. 121f. and in a wider context the study by June Singer, *Androgyny: The Opposites Within*. In process-oriented thinking, as exemplified by rDzogs-chen thought, there is no sharp separation between opposites whose overcoming remains precarious, there is only complementarity in which the opposites include each other and thereby give meaning to each other.

54. I emphasize *early* because the later rDzogs-chen form of thought as represented by Klong-chen rab-'byams-pa is quite different in many respects.

55. It is important to bear in mind the distinction between *slob-dpon* "instructor" and/or *slob-dpon chen-po* "great instructor" and *ston-pa*, both of which allow themselves to be rendered as "teacher." In rDzogs-chen thought the term *ston-pa* does not refer to any concrete person. It intimates a higher order reality with its principle of "information." By contrast, *slob-dpon* is used in connection with a human person. In order to avoid misconceptions, I render *slob-dpon* by "instructor" and *ston-pa* by "teacher."

56. His "biography" is a composite of Judaic, Christian, Iranian, and Indian themes and legends: the Annunciation by the angel Gabriel to the Virgin Mary, the appearance of a translucent person before the Virgin Sudharmā, placing a crystal box on her head, the appearance of the sun god before the Virgin Kuntī and begetting on her Karṇa, one of the heroes in the Indian *Mahābhārata*; the exposure of the "unwanted" child and its rescue (the story of Moses) fused with the notion of the Resurrection of Christ, which in the case of dGa'-rab rdo-rje prompted his aliases Ro-lang bde-ba (The one who is happy in having risen from the dead) and Ro-lang thal-mdog (the one who has the color of ashes in having risen from the dead), only to mention a few instances. In between dGa'-rab rdo-rje as the earliest rDzogs-chen instructor and Padmasambhava as the latest figure in early rDzogs-chen, the abbot from China (*rgya-nag-gi mkhan-po*) Śrīsiṃha is mentioned. For some time he was active in Li-yul (Khotan) and, accordimg to Klong-chen rab-'byams-pa (*gNas-lugs*, p. 68), he was the Hva-shang, so much maligned by the later bKa'-brgyud-pa and dGe-lugs-pa sects.

57. Literally translated Dhanakośa means "Treasury of Wealth"; and wealth flowed along the Silk Route, be this the northern (Kucha) or southern (Khotan) route.

58. There is no evidence for either Alexander Cunningham's or Giuseppe Tucci's identification of Uḍḍiyāna with the Swat Valley in Pakistan. On the contrary, all the evidence points to Central Asia south of the Aral Sea. What they overlook or deliberately ignore is the unanimously accepted tradition of Padmasambhava's birthplace being associated with a lake and the overwhelming frequency of the ending, -*ana* in Central Asian place names, for instance, Sogdhiana, Drangiana, Ferghana, and so on, and even the name Urgensch (see Edgar Knobloch, *Beyond the Oxus*, p. 73). It therefore seems to be more reasonable to connect his birthplace with Sogdhiana, situated around Lake Aral, and to take note of the fact

that the Sogdhians were highly educated people whose religion "was a synthesis of many creeds and currents, incorporating elements of Zoroastrianism, Manichaeism, Buddhism, and Christianity, together with Greek and Indian mythology. Trade with China was entirely in their hands and their outposts and settlements were scattered practically all over Chinese Turkestan" (Edgar Knobloch, *Beyond the Oxus*, p. 54). This synthesis, if not so say, syncretism is quite evident in Padmasambhava's own writings. It is more than likely that, when the Sogdhian civilization was crushed by the Arabs, he came as a "refugee" to Tibet and, in order to protect his relatives, who were left behind, declared himself to have neither a father nor a mother.

59. *Ri-bo brtsegs-pa'i rgyud* (sDe-dge ed., vol. 3, fols. 1–12b), fol. 4b. These two movements stem from the whole's energy pervaded homogeneity or principle of self-consistency (*mnyam-pa*) as this text states:

In the whole's energy pervaded homogeneity
It is from its ecstatic intensity (*rig-pa*) or loss in intensity (*ma-rig-pa*)
That (its) upward unfolding (*yar rgyas*) or downward going astray
(*mar 'khrul*) comes to pass.

On the meaning of the important term(s) *mnyam-pa/mnyam-nyid* see note 14. Both movements reflect the whole's understanding (*rtogs*) or lack of understanding (*ma-rtogs*) itself, both of which are the overt expressions of the whole's ecstatic intensity or loss in intensity, respectively. Hence, both movements are holistic in the sense that the one leads to greater and more intense wholeness, while the other leads to a diminished or fragmented wholeness. In this respect, the two movements differ from our ascent and descent whose connotations are too "individualistic." The consequences of the whole's lack of understanding itself and, by implication, of our lack of understanding what we really are have been summed up by Padmasambhava in his *Nyi-zla'i snying-po*, fol. 39a:

The (whole's) lack of understanding (its) energy creates pitfalls for
itself;
The (whole's) lack of understanding (its) primal symbolicalness lets
(itself) become shrouded;
The (whole's) not holding to its legitimate dwelling lets it go astray
into the six kinds of living beings.

Behind this aphoristic statement lies Padmasambhava's triune process "ontology" of wholeness (Being-in-its-beingness), that is, the whole's energy is its *thinking* of thinking (*sems-nyid*), its primal symbolicalness is its *lumen naturale* (*'od-gsal*), and its legitimate dwelling is its unorigination (*skye-med*), in other words, wholeness, whether we look at it from the perspective of its *thinking* of thinking or its symbolicalness is not something that "happens," but just is. Padmasambhava's and the later rDzogs-chen thinkers' insistence on understanding or, should we say, on an *inner* standing, on us as human individuals being a self-regulatory (autopoietic) process, sets rDzogs-chen thought apart from all other speculative (rational-reductionist) systems that absolutize specific preference and merely juggle with opposites without ever coming closer to the source from which the opposites have sprung. It is not by blindly engaging in actions decreed good or renouncing actions decreed evil (of which procedure Padmasambhava, *Nyi-zla'i snying-po*, fol. 36b, says that it means first to engage deliberately in evil actions and then to rationalize them away), that we grow into our humanity; we do so through an understanding/*inner* standing that is available *within* ourselves. Padmasambhava's ideas echoed in the statement (*mKha'-'gro snying-thig* [abbr.: *mKha'-snying*], vol. 1, pp. 348, 486):

> Without having done the slightest good Kun-tu bzang-po, through the intensity of his supraconscious awareness of what the triadic loss of intensity involves, has (grown into) spiritual wakefulness (*sangs-rgyas*); without having done the slightest evil, through their lacking in this supraconscious awareness, the sentient beings in the triad world system roam about in this world system

is in all likelihood also meant as a critique of the Gnostics' obsession with "sin" and the "Fall."

60. This has been neatly summed up in an epitaph on one of the wayside crucifixes in the Austrian Alps I saw many years ago. Its translation from the Tyrolian dialect in which it was written reads as follows:

> It took him five hours to climb to the top of the mountain;
> It took him five seconds to come down.
> Up there he was alive and in the best of health;
> Down here he is dead and gone.

61. Following Erich Jantsch, *Design for Evolution*, I mean by "mythological" the feedback link between the experiencer and the forces that work in and through him/her—"projected" outward in images with which the experiencer establishes a personal relationship; by "psychological," I mean the subtle interplay of physical-emotional and imaginal-spiritual factors in the whole person.

62. *Nyi-zla'i snying-po*, fol. 44a.

63. According to Padmasambhava, *Nyi-zla'i snying-po*, fol 44a, there are five such doors, each door presenting one fossilized aspect of the whole of Buddhism in its ritual practices and intellectual pursuits.

64. By "thinking," I do not mean the restrictivenes of representational thought. Rather, thinking is, in Heideggerian terms, a "seeing in an exceptional sense," and the "seer" is, as Michael David Levin, *The Opening of Vision*, p. 454, clearly states: "One who exemplifies in some way an individual—that is to say, self-individuating—realization of the human potential, the human capacity to see".

65. They are called *"spyi-ti"* and *"yang-ti"* respectively. They are not dealt with in any Western works on Buddhism.

66. *Nyi-zla'i snying-po*, fol. 44a.

67. A mere glance at this verse in its original Tibetan version reveals an abundance of highly technical terms that are concepts by intuition, not by postulation, which makes their rendering extremely difficult if one has not had the experience which they attempt to convey. We have already met the terms *snang-gsal* "the glare of the phenomenal" and *chos-sku* "the fore-structure (of one's individuation)"; so it suffices to refer to notes 49 and 50 above, respectively. The term *zang-thal*, used in connection with *snang-gsal*, defies any analytical or intellectual definition; it "names" what can only be experienced and only inadequately put into words that are geared to the requirements of material life. The rendering of this term by "dissipating into nothing" attempts to convey something of the experience a person may have had at one time or another in his life and most often in what is reported as a near-death experience, when everything gross falls off and one walks right through a wall into what is called "infinity." In his *Nyi-zla'i snying-po*, fol. 24b, Padmasambhava explicates *zang-thal* as follows:

The five senses and their five objects are what constitutes the
     essence of (the whole's) errancy mode ('*khrul-pa*),
The non-existence of the ego-logical mode (of their dealing with
     their objects, '*dzin-med*) is (what is meant by) dissipating into
     nothing, the repulsion of the errancy mode;

and in his *sPros-bral don-gsal*, fols. 73b f., he explicates *zang-thal* in connection with the lighting-up of the whole's originary awareness modes as follows:

Since the manner in which the originary awareness modes light up
has neither an exteriority nor an interiority these modes are said to
be *zang-thal*.

Both *skye-med* and *ka-dag* are terms describing an ontological experience. In *skye-med* the emphasis is on *med* "nonexistent," which is not the same as "being without" which implies two "things" both of which "exist" independent of each other. And this is precisely what Padmasambhava rejects. In a similar vein Padmasambhava elucidates the term *ka-dag* in his *Rin-po-che spyi-gnad skyon-sel thig-le kun-gsal-gyi rgyud* (sDe-dge ed., vol. 2, fols.313a–315b), fol. 315a, as follows:

> *ka-dag* means that (what is so referred to) has from the onset of its originary presencing (*ye-nas*) been uncontaminated by the mire of the obscuring and veiling (activity of the intellect) and the organismic forces as well as by the darkness of a low-level conscious intensity and by the mire of the instinctual-emotional.

Actually, as Padmasambhava himself had stated earlier (*sPyi-gnad skyon-sel*, fol. 314(ii)b), what is intended by any of these technical terms cannot be expressed in words. To speak of them is only meant to enable people of low intelligence to get some inkling of its significance. The term *ka-dag*, pointing to an experience of a supraordinate clarity that is primal (*ka*), is closely related to what is described as *dag-snang*, expressing what Ernst Cassirer had called "symbolic pregnance." See also note 49.

68. On the important distinction between totality and wholeness see David Michael Levin, *The Opening of Vision*, pp. 79, 176, 455.

69. See note 9 for a tentative translation of the technical term *thig-le nyag-gcig*.

70. Into the assumption of being some thing, we are led by our language that has locked us firmly into a metaphysical trap. The use of the article (definite or indefinite) turns what follows into a noun and nouns stand for things, be they real or imaginal.

71. Gnostic thinkers had an inkling of this fact when they talked about the *pleroma*, an idea revived by the late psychologist C. G. Jung in his *Septem Sermones ad Mortuos*. For a detailed study of the strictly gnostic idea see Kurt Rudolph, *Gnosis*, pp. 320f.

72. The Tibetan term is *"sbubs"* which means a "sheath," an "envelope," suggesting, from a dynamic perspective, the image of the whole wrapping itself about itself, each such movement presenting a diminished energy level with fewer and fewer possibilities. There are according to Padmasambhava's *sPros-bral don-gsal*, fols. 71b f., three such "sheaths." The first is the *rin-chen sbubs* "the sheath of preciousness" that in its transparency is likened to a crystal that, as our second story shows, is a a symbol of a human person's individuation process whose "program" or fore-structure is the *chos-sku*. The second sheath is called "*'od-kyi sbubs,*" "the sheath of light" that in its iridescence is the function (*ye-shes*) of the structure (*sku*) and "sets up" a pattern of communion (*longs-sku*) and has much in common with what is known as a person's "aura"—"the raiment of light" as David Tansley calls the aura in his study bearing the title *The*

Raiment of Light. The third sheath is called *"bag-chags sbubs,"* "the sheath of inveterate tendencies"—the sedimentations of our cognitive and emotional experiences whose concreteness prevents us from seeing them as dynamic patterns (*sprul-sku*).

73. The terms *sku* and *lus* are closely related, each pointing to different, yet coordinated, if not to say, intermeshing levels in experience. This difference I try to indicate by using the word "gestalt" or "fore-structure" as the context demands for *sku* and the word "body" in its biological (psychophysical) complexity for *lus*. In the Buddhist context this intermeshing has been concisely stated in *Bi-ma snying-thig*, vol. 2, p. 444. In the Western context this insight into the difference between Gestalt and Körper, Leib, Fleisch has been captured, to the best of my knowledge, by the German poet Novalis (Friedrich von Hardenberg) in his *Fragmente* n. 1325:

Es gibt nur einen Tempel in der Welt, und das ist der menschliche Körper. Nichts ist heiliger als diese hehre Gestalt. Das Bücken vor Menschen ist eine Huldigung dieser Offenbarung im Fleisch. Man berührt den Himmel, wenn man einen Menschenleib betastet.

There is only *one* temple in the world, and this is the human body. Nothing is more sacred than this sublime Gestalt. To bow down before human beings is to pay homage to this revelation in the flesh. One touches heaven when one caresses a human body.

It may not be out of place to point out that, after two millenia of vilification of the body and contempt of the flesh in the Christian West, they now are gradually regaining their rightful place and legitimate dignity. In this respect, the writings of the philosopher Maurice Merleau-Ponty have been influential. Toward the end of his life he replaced the term "corporeal schema" by "flesh." For further details about the resurrection of the flesh see David Michael Levin, *The Body's Recollection of Being*, s.v.; *The Opening of Vision*, s.v.; *The Listening Self*, s.v.

74. See for instance Klong-chen rab-'byams-pa's *mThar-thug 'od-kyi snying-po* (in: *Zab-yang*, vol. 1, pp. 293–307), p. 294.

75. *sPros-bral don-gsal*, fol. 5a.

76. *zer* "ray of light" and *zer* "to speak" are homonyms.

77. In this context, see the deeply probing study of David Michael Levin, *The Listening Self*; also Joachim-Ernst Berendt, *The Third Ear*.

78. Ibid., p. 765.

79. *Nyi-zla'i snying-po*, fol. 21a.

80. The same argument applies to the Buddhist equivalent *thugs* that refers to the *thinking* of thinking, not to mentation *(sems)* or "mind" in Western terminology, from which *thugs* is always clearly distinguished. In order to bring out the dynamic character of this *thinking* of thinking, the terms *dgongs-(pa)* and *thugs-dgongs* are used. *dgongs* may be rendered as "design" in the sense that as an integral aspect of wholeness it intimates that wholeness designs its own evolution and meaning.

81. This is implied by the term *snang-srid*, a compound that reflects the binary mode of ordinary thinking: outside/inside, matter/mind, samsara/nirvana and so on. In his *sNang-srid kha-sbyor bdud-rtsi bcud-thigs*, Padmasambhava has taken up this problem and has introduced *kha-sbyor* (literally "joining mouths," whatever literalness may be worth) as a ternary term by which he, in the last analysis, understands Being (in his diction the Being-that-is-not).

82. *chos-can.* See *Nyi-zla'i snying-po*, fols. 19b and 22a: *chos-can snang-srid sna-tshogs.* On fol. 20a these logical constructs are understood as the rays of light to which the creativity in Being's energy, as its luminosity, manifests itself.

83. Strictly speaking, the terms *chos-nyid*, which I have rendered as "Being's possibilizing dynamics" or "Being's internal logic," depending on the context, and *chos-can*, literally meaning "that which is of the nature of thought," here rendered as "logical construct," belong to the language of logic with which Buddhist thought, in the course of time, became ever more identified and, as a consequence, impoverished. Padmasambhava seems to have understood *chos-nyid* in the sense in which Johann Wolfgang von Goethe spoke of Faust's concern:

Dass ich erkenne, was die Welt
Im Innersten zusammenhält
So that I discern what, deep within,
Bonds the universe.

(*Faust*, "Night," part I, vs. 382–383)

84. *Nyi-zla'i snying-po*, fol. 30a.

85. *sngon-thog.* For an elucidation of this compound of *sngon* and *thog-(ma)* see above p. 21 n. 28. It may not be out of place to quote in connection with this passage and its insistence on Being's internal logic what the German poet Novalis (Friedrich von Hardenberg) has to say about a "beginning" (*Fragmente*, no. 423):

Aller wirklicher Anfang ist ein zweiter Moment. Alles was da ist, erscheint, ist und erscheint nur unter einer Voraussetzung: sein indi-

vidueller Grund, sein absolutes Selbst geht ihm voraus, muss wenigstens vor ihm gedacht *werden*

Every real beginning is a second moment. Everything that exists, appears, exists and appears only under one presupposition: its individual ground, its absolute Self precedes it, must at least be *thought* before it. [emphasis mine]

86. As a matter of fact, "intellect" (*blo*) as the exclusively rational approach to life's mystery and "failure to understand" (*ma-rtogs*) are synonymous for him. See *Nyi-zla'i snying-po*, fol. 43a. Condensing and rephrasing his lengthy dissertation in modern terms, we can say that if you expect answers to your question about life's mystery and meaning from the rational approach, you will get all the fictions it can concoct or facts it can construct. When it comes to understanding, your very question may have become redundant.

87. *Nyi-zla'i snying-po*, fols. 42b–43a.

ONE

Abduction and Deliverance

The mystery of the ultimate inseparability of the external and the internal of which poets and mystics all over the world have had a vision that deeply moved them, has been expressed in the Western world with great sensibility by the German Romantic poet Friedrich von Hardenberg, known as Novalis (1772–1801). Twice in his *Fragmente* he returns to this vision. The first statement reads as follows:

> *Das Äussre ist gleichsam nur ein verteiltes, übersetztes Innre, ein höheres Innre.*
> The external, it seems, is only a distributed, transposed internal, a higher internal.[1]

The second statement reads:

> *Das Äussre ist ein in Geheimniszustand erhobnes Innre. (Vielleicht auch umgekehrt.)*
> The external is the internal raised to a level of mystery; Maybe it's also the other way round.[2]

While the "mystery" impels us to probe its secrets without ever becoming less "mysterious," its being a "higher internal" suggests a hierarchical organization in what remains an undivided whole. In this unity of a deeply felt and ever present mystery and a higher order level as an interpretation of it, human creativity is rooted. Storytelling is one of its absorbing manifestations, all of which point to a dimension beyond themselves. This dimension is, in popular psycholog-

35

ical jargon, the "unconscious"[3] as an ever active matrix, not as a mere container, of archetypal patterns coming to life in our body-based feelings that blend with the images of our imagination as a humanly unique means to come to know ourselves in our wholeness. And what these images and feelings "tell" us is the story of how this process of self-realization and individuation unfolds in the experiencer. The manner in which they tell their story is exceedingly cryptic and often very abrupt. There are disconcerting gaps we must fill with our imagination. This means that we cannot simply stand aside and watch the story unfold by itself, but at every stage have to participate in its unfolding.

The theme of the first story is the luring and making prisoner an individual's spirit in the barren and narrow ravines of earthly existence, its descent, and the extricating of itself from its cell with the help of friends, but primarily by itself. It is preserved in two versions, the one stylistically very abrupt,[4] the other slightly smoother,[5] but both are alike in reflecting the narrator's aim to instill a sense of wonder in the listener.[6] In the context in which the story is told, the narrator is none other than the archetypal figure of the Self acting as teacher,[7] and the listener is the assemblage of ethereal *anima*-like figures[8] who have asked the teacher to elucidate by way of an allegory to them the theme of an individual's (humankind's) becoming enworlded and of his/her (its) regaining his/her (its) original wholeness through a process of individuation. The story is deceptively simple in its presentation, but actually moves simultaneously on three intermeshing levels (the worldly-external, the psychic-internal, and the mystic-existential or arcane one) and, on the reader's or listener's part, presupposes a familiarity with concepts and images that, for the most part, have been accessible only to a few "initiates." The story runs as follows:

> Once upon a time, in the country of Yangs-pa-can[9] there lived a teacher by the name of 'Od-'gyed-pa.[10] There also were two blood-related boys.

[By disloyal friends][11] they were held captive in a desolate ravine.

Then five soldiers appeared and razed the stone castle from top to bottom.

When the two boys had been put into a dungeon, an old woman called Ling-tog-can[12] locked the door.

Then four persons ["insiders"] pursued and grappled with the five mounted soldiers whom they unhorsed.

The two boys set themselves free and killed the jailers.

At once they ran away to the [castle] Nyi-ma-can[13] in the distance, and when they had collected the taxes from the populace, they were counselled by twenty-one court-ladies and conducted into a [precious] inner sanctum from which worldly thoughts had been excluded. Five doormen bearing shields guarded the door so that nobody could enter.

Then the four (afore mentioned) persons looked at their faces in four mirrors and recognized themselves for what they were.

Then they saw that the one room had eight doors and they smiled at each other and their laughter became ever more wondrous.

The following analysis and explication is based on scattered glosses in the original text itself, on additional glosses and paraphrases by Klong-chen rab-'byams-pa and rGod-kyi ldem-'phru-can, and on relevant passages from the vast body of rDzogs-chen literature whose salient ideas ultimately go back to Padmasambhava whose primary concern is the evolutionary dynamic of human existence.

A mere glance at this short story shows that it is marked by an abundance of male personages who, whether singly or in distinct groups, converge on the central duo, the blood-related boys. Only at a later stage a number of female figures begin to play a significant role.

There is first of all the lone teacher who, as his name implies, is of the nature of a suprasensible light that he radiates or in whose luster he is ablaze. His residence is a country with the name that literally means "being of the nature of presenting a vast expanse" and subtly intimates the immensity of (an individual's) external and internal dimensions. In both the images of the teacher and his residence, the emphasis is on the attributes of their being luminous and being vast, rather than on their personification and reification. This emphasis at once lifts them out of the ordinary without negating the latter. Both the teacher and his residence are "features" in a fivefold complexity—the other three "features" being the audience, the message, and the temporariness—whose ontogenetic transformations extend over three or four—depending on how one counts—hierarchically coordinated levels.[14]

Throughout the history of Buddhist thought, increasingly focusing on the timeless and acausal, psychospiritual aspects of the individual, the teacher has been a guiding image of paramount importance.[15] In this image, the (material) sociocultural[16] and (immaterial) spiritual levels in which every living individual shares, interpenetrate dynamically. The guiding image of the teacher is felt to have a kind of magnetic pull that draws and leads anyone who carefully listens into a dimension of spiritual enrichment and fulfilment. In the form of a humanly recognizable teacher, this suprasensible light, the *lumen naturale*, as it was once experienced and called,[17] not only makes us aware of the fact that the universe is alight and human in essence, but also of the fact that within each of us this light is shining as the inner light of humanness. Though not concretely identifiable, this inner light can be experienced intuitively and in an ecstatic originary manner deep within ourselves, where it is present "self-originated" and "lying beyond the reach of our rational/analytical causality-dominated thinking."[18] The intensity of this suprasensible light is inseparable from its "field" that corresponds to the intensity that passes through and occupies it. In the form of the teacher, it spreads the light of spiritual values throughout the country in which the teacher resides as that country's light.

In the conventional context, the teacher is the historical Buddha and the country is the ancient Vaiśālī/Vessālī whose name the Tibetans translated as Yangs-pa-can, "a country of immense tracts of land." In the spiritual context, this immensity is the "inner immensity" of the whole's internal logic as which its possibilizing dynamics expresses itself.[19] Its presence in us is sensed *in-tuitively* (perceived from within) as presenting a palace that in its vastness is a country, illimitable like the sky in its vortex-like movement and the birthplace of our experienceable world.[20] The intertwining of this possibilizing dynamics and the gestalt character this "thinking" assumes in becoming the fore-structure of our (meaning-rich) individuated being has been beautifully depicted by Padmasambhava:

> The presencing of Being's internal logic as the fore-structure (of its evolution), is like the sun's (reflection) in a mirror; Being's internal logic becoming engulfed by the fore-structure (of its evolution) is like (the inter-meshing of milk and butter; the energy of Being's internal logic residing in its supraconscious ecstatic intensity is like the sun in the sky; the splitting of Being's undivided internal logic into the creative dynamics in the fore-structure (of its evolution) is like a razor's back and its cutting-edge.[21]

At some time the inner immensity of Being's possibilizing dynamics and its formulation into an intuitively perceptible gestalt was linked with the container metaphor of a flask whose contents retain an ever-youthful freshness.[22] As a "felt" image or, what amounts to the same, an "imaged" feeling, this inner immensity in the shape of a cornucopia-like flask not only intimates by its perceptible form the ever-present supraconscious ecstatic intensity of the whole's spirit/spirituality that it expresses and of which it is its expression,[23] but also instills in the experiencer the feeling of being enfolded in a precious sheath or envelope[24] that is the perceptible and existentially felt meaning of wholeness, pre-

sent in us as the fore-structure of our individuation process.[25]
This inner immensity, under whatever image it may be experienced, is in later rDzogs-chen diction a "spontaneous thereness," a "just is"[26] that serves as the starting point (or, should
we say the "platform" because of its field character?) from
which the universe (including the human individual) unfolds.
It is similar to rays of light that burst forth from a crystal in
multicolored brilliance. The immensity of this spontaneous
thereness is simultaneously "out there" and "in here"; out
there, it is the country Yangs-pa-can in this story, in here it is
the whole's possibilizing dynamics (in Padmasambhava's terminology) and the supraconscious ecstatic intensity that is
known to itself in its experience by us (in Klong-chen rab-
'byams-pa's diction). In two beautiful stanzas, Klong-chen
rab-'byams-pa elaborates the unity of the three fore-structures as programs of our individuation into the existentiality
of our humanness and Being's spontaneous thereness:[27]

> Though the five (rays of) light may each have their
>   specific color
> When from a crystal the light (in it) bursts forth
>   incessantly,
> There is nothing good or evil about them, they are the
>   creative dynamics in a single crystal;
> (So) the supraconscious ecstatic intensity that is known
>   to itself in the beingness of (its and our) Being is
>   similar to a crystal:
> Its openness/nothingness is what is said to be the fore-
>   structure (of the individuation process),
> Its brilliance, an inner glow (shining in and by itself) is
>   the program (or fore-structure) of its communion
>   (with the whole's evolutionary field character), and
> The doors that stand incessantly open to what is the
>   ground and reason for there being (a) world (to be
>   envisioned) are (the fore-structures of) the guiding
>   images (that lead us through the maze of our
>   enworldedness).[28]

Throughout the time of Being coming-to-the-fore
Its pure and primal symbolicalness, the three programs
   (and fore-structures of our existentiality) as the self-
   manifestations of (Being's Buddhahood), and
Its opacity, the whole of the (environing) world and the
   organisms (in it)
Are in themselves as the triad of nothingness, brilliance,
   and multiplicity
The play (staged) by the fore-structure of the
   individuation process, the fore-structure of its
   unfoldedness in (the whole's) contextuality, and the
   fore-structure of its guiding images.
This triad of programs (that structure our
   existentiality), Being's presencing in its playfulness
   and creativity,
Is in its self-manifestation a spontaneous thereness and
   need not be looked for elsewhere.
Still one has to distinguish between (the two modes[29] of
   Being's self-manifestation) and understand
That the (dull) things called samsara and nirvana and
   the (bright) realms (constituted by) the three
   programs (in) Being's spontaneous thereness
Are the dimension of our spiritual quest.

The implication of these two stanzas is that in the strictly human context, the human individual can create him/herself and a world in which he/she can live through a process of individuation prefigured by the three programs already existing in him/her as possibilities. In other words, these three programs, with their wealth of qualities, structure the individuation process and act like guiding images with whom the traveller of this road can establish a personal relationship by seeing in them his or her teacher who is thus none else but the whole's *lumen naturale* energizing every aspect of the individual's individuation process and quest. This *lumen naturale* in its threefold radiation is, as Padmasambhava noted long ago, the teacher of us in our existential reality:[30]

The teacher of our existential reality is (the whole's)
   ternary (anthropic) dynamics,[31]
Unagitated and uncalculating it resides (in us).[32]

Quite abruptly our story now introduces two blood-related boys. Nothing is said about their parents and it is left to the imagination of the listener to see them as "tangible" replicas of the "intangible" light that is the teacher. If this is the case, the subtle shift from the "one" light to "two" luminous presences intimates a break in the original unity, the triune intensity of the whole.[33] Both boys are of the nature of light and whatever happens to the light happens to both. Then, how does it happen that disaster strikes and the light is captured in the vicissitudes of its having become enworlded but, in the end, extricates itself unscathed?

rGod-kyi ldem-'phru-can speaks of "disloyal friends" and thereby intimates that the disaster is brought about by persons close to the sufferers, not by total strangers. These disloyal friends soon reappear as five mounted soldiers[34] who raze to the ground the castle from which the boys had been lured away, and by this act of violence complete their earlier betrayal. The characterization of these negative forces as disloyal friends and, subsequently, as violent soldiers suggests that they were understood as aspects of a psychic whole, revealing an inner tension in the intrinsic inseparability of the two blood-related boys who, in Jungian terms, can be said to stand in a compensatory and complementary relationship of shadow (the "darker" side of the psyche) and persona (the "brighter" side of the psyche with which our ego tends to identify).[35] However, as Padmasambhava has informed us, these blood-related boys—in a wider sense "children" of a single "mother"—are the concrete expressions of the rays of light that spreads from the "Being-as-fundamental-forces"[36] aspect of Being in the lighting-up of its creative dynamics.[37] This lighting-up itself is at risk to be taken for something other than what it is and on this basis Padmasambhava can also say that the boys or children, in general, are.already mistaken identifications of the rays of light branching out from the whole's (Being's) creative dynamics.[38]

This emphasis on the creative dynamics of Being, whether we conceive of Being's intensity in terms of Being's possibilizing dynamics (as is done by Padmasambhava) or a supraconscious ecstatic intensity (as is done by Klong-chen rab-'byams-pa) answers the question why disaster should strike. Being's creative dynamics never allows itself to be "at rest." This "never-being-at-rest" expresses itself in a complementarity that, following Klong-chen rab-'byams-pa, is imaged as Kun-tu bzang-po (the male aspect) and Kun-tu bzang-mo (the female aspect).[39] These aspects as formulated energies or intensities already constitute a symmetry break in the original and undivided wholeness and simultaneously prefigure the emergence of human life in the concrete. This primal complementarity, humankind's archetypal disposition to becoming human in a non-fragmentary manner, functions through another complementarity technically known as the effectiveness principle and the discrimination-appreciation principle. Appreciation, in particular, is an intensification of the cognitive capacity that pervades all life and, in Jungian terms, is the *archetype of life itself*.[40] It is "She" who is eager to experience and test whatever can be known—in principle everything can be known, depending on what we understand by "knowing." In her (its) eagerness, she (appreciation) is like a racehorse rushing in the direction of the maze presented by the welter of what can be known, the knowable.[41] In this mad pursuit, in the absence of which life would be intolerably boring, a turbulence is created[42] and the "quietness" of the sheer lucency of the original complementarity, Kun-tu bzang-po and Kun-tu bzang-mo absorbed in each other in their intimate embrace, is destroyed by it and disorder seems to prevail. The once uniform sheer lucency is broken up into a prismatic display of colors.[43] In this disruption, *cognition*, as we commonly understand this word, is born. This means that to disrupt is to know and to know is to disrupt, but this, in turn, also causes confusion[44] and with it a feeling of being lost in some no man's land—"the desolate ravine" of the story.

Now, to make the plight of the forlorn boys even worse, five mounted soldiers appear and, as noted before, their first act of violence is to raze to the ground the castle that once seemed so strong because it was a stone structure, rather than an adobe hovel. These soldiers, who form a set of five, are a person's untamed libido, the instinctual-affective forces that more often than not have devastating effects.[45] They are, in the traditional order of their enumeration, passion as the ego's urge to possess what it desires, resentment toward whatever impedes our covetous inclination, arrogance as the ego's disposition claiming for itself an unwarranted importance, envy as the narrowness of our ego-centric perspective, and the abysmal darkness of spiritual blindness and stupidity.[46]

Once the soldiers have destroyed the home of the two boys they put them into a dungeon. In Buddhist texts, the dungeon or prison has been a favorite symbol for samsara, this dismal place where the individual's myopic ego-logical concern with and involvement in the things-at-hand do not allow for the unfoldment of originary awareness modes whose objective reference, to use a term properly belonging to epistemology rather than to visionary experiences, is the lighting-up of what there is or to become in an unearthly luminosity. In the darkness of a dungeon, the imprisoned individual's originary awareness modes cannot spread their radiance, neither has the supraconscious ecstatic intensity of which the originary awareness modes are functions any scope, nor can the experiencer's appreciative acumen curl up in the bare aliveness of its appreciated "object."[47] But not only is the dungeon of samsara constructed by the instinctual-affective forces, it also is the soil from which they grow and proliferate. In a beautiful simile a gloss in the text compares their excessive growth with the proliferation of leaves on a plant that thereby is prevented from bearing any fruits (as every gardener knows).

The final act in this drama features an old woman who firmly locks the door of the dungeon so that an escape is

made well-nigh impossible. Her name *ling-tog-can*, "afflicted
with amaurosis" or, more in line with the tenor of this story,
"She who is of the nature of amaurosis," is highly descriptive.[48] How does she fit into the almost all-male pattern of
the story and why is she an old woman? She is old because
she belongs to the oldest stratum in what we have come to
call "mind"—a vague, ill-defined and, maybe, undefinable
concept—, which as organismic mentation is primarily
instinctual-affective; she even encompasses all the other
instinctual-affective forces and thus may be spoken of as
their matrix and be counted as a "sixth" instinctual-affective
force.[49] She is a woman because she is of the nature of Being's
supraconscious cognitiveness that in its openness/nothing-
ness is a sheer intensity allowing other intensities to pass over
its field-like character, except that she has not yet become the
supraconscious ecstatic intensity that as spirit/spirituality
reaches into each of us embodied beings as (the whole's)
effectiveness principle in its quality of tenderness/gentleness
due to its fusion with (the whole's) openness/nothingness in
its quality of "appreciation" (intuition, inspiration) and in
this unity constituting (the whole's) dynamics as its *lumen
naturale* present in each of us. There is nothing or hardly
anything of this light about her and, having remained on the
level of the instinctual-affective which, too, is cognitive to a
degree, she is aptly spoken of as "She who is not quite supraconscious ecstatic intensity."[50]

In this desperate situation, four persons appear on the
scene and start grappling with the five mounted soldiers
whom they unhorse. But why is there this seeming discrepancy of only four against five? Again, it is rGod-kyi ldem-
'phru-can who gives us a clue by pointing out that they are
"insiders." This means that, like the disloyal friends who
lured the blood-related boys from their home, they are close
to these boys whom they assist in extricating themselves out
of their predicament. In a sense, they are the other side of the
disloyal friends, integral aspects of the boys' cognitive capacity that itself is the creative dynamics in the supraconscious

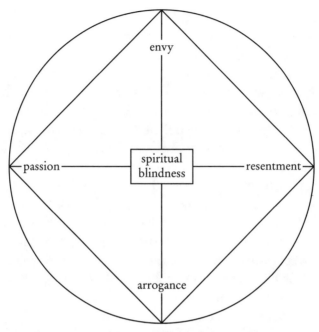

Figure 1.1. *The geometry of the instinctual-emotional.* Experientially *this geometry becomes alive with resentment and passion as complementary to each other, reinforced by arrogance and envy.*

ecstatic intensity[51] and, as such, is a symbol for the authentic Self's wholeness. All this goes to show that life cannot go further and "higher up" before having gone downward. Still, the difference in numbers has to be accounted for. The story itself does not say how many disloyal friends there were in the first place. However, we can safely assume that there were four. Once they had abducted the two boys and turned the "brighter" aspect of them in the already existent "darker" aspect and thus converted the two boys into another "shadowy" member of their gang, the resultant number is five. Psychologically speaking, the Self has been forced into the role of the ego that in its spiritual blindness participates in the destruction of the castle from which it as the Self had been abducted. The resultant ego-logical and ego-centric, instinctual and affective situation can be diagrammed in the form of a *maṇḍala*, a centered four,[52] as in Figure 1.1.

In view of the fact that a *maṇḍala* is basically a static geo-metric structure it admirably depicts the rigidity and narrow-ness of an individual's ego-logical perspective that by necessity is averse to a visionary opening-up.

The arrival of four persons and their grappling with the five soldiers marks the ascendency of the discriminative/apprecia-tive-spiritual over the instinctual-affective. As "insiders"—we might even say as "loyal friends" and helpers—they stand in a much closer relationship to the Self, the whole's supra-conscious ecstatic intensity, than the instinctual-affective that only too often is an adversary to the spiritual and hence is so aptly and summarily spoken of a "disloyal friends." Yet, in the personalistic diction of the text, the spiritual and the instinctual are said to be "blood-related boys" who implicitly need each other.[53] That is to say, in order to become truly self-reflexive and spiritually conscious, the spiritual needs the instinctual-affective from which it differentiates itself by means of an "appreciative acumen" dynamics, forming a fourfold, a quaternary disposition to wholeness that tacitly accentuates its center from which it branches out and to which it returns.[54]

Simultaneously with the ascendency of the spiritual over the instinctual-affective, prompted by an energy influx through the arrival of the four insiders, the "brighter" side of the whole's dynamics, the center or two-as-one is roused out of the one-sidedness of its lethargy and spiritual blindness and as a renewed intensity takes an active part in its becoming restored to its original wholeness.

The first "insider" is the "appreciative acumen that sets free."[55] What it sets free is the whole's inner dynamics that had become distorted into the instinctual-affective. By releasing this dynamics, it purifies it from its accumulated dross and translates and transforms it into a realm of sym-bolic forms.[56] This setting free is a recovery and re-discovery of what the instinctual-affective really is by recognizing and appreciating its vital role in providing otherwise neglected insight and creative impulses. Each of the multiple manifestations of the instinctual-affective in the form of a specific emotion is the presence of the whole's originary awareness in some misplaced concreteness[57] whose inflexibility is responsible for irresistible drives and compulsive ideas that are the very opposite of insight and creativity. In so being set free through the appreciative acumen's recognition of its "psychic-spiritual" quality, the instinctual-affective begins to play an active role in the symbolic re-creation of reality. The instinctual-affective turns negative only when it is not recognized for what it is, that is, psychic energy, and is repressed by the ego's claim to sole supremacy, itself an *idée fixe* which it does not recognize for what it is.

The second "insider" is the "appreciative acumen that gathers."[58] What it gathers is the radiation-dominated (luminous) aspect of the fundamental forces that together with the matter-dominated (opaque) aspect is active in building up the physical (though not "nothing-but" physical) universe of which every living being is an integral part.[59] The light in these forces that had been set free by the preceding appreciative acumen is now "gathered" in the whole's widening dimension shimmering in five luminosities that are, strictly speaking, the whole's proto-lighting of what ordinary perception perceives in its shining-out as colors.[60] This proto-lighting presents a challenge to the "seeing" experiencer. As an "as if" of which more will be said later, it is hermeneutically disclosive; as a light assuming a distinct color, it is reductionist-assertive and likely to draw the experiencer back into the confines of ordinary perception from which the first appreciative acumen had redeemed him. Utmost attention is needed to differentiate between these two modes of a mere perceiving and an actual "seeing."[61]

This differentiation that is as much discrimination as it is an opening-up is effected by the third "insider," the "appreciative acumen that separates."[62] What it separates is that which is not quite the supraconscious ecstatic intensity and the supraconscious ecstatic intensity, the instinctual-affective and the discriminative-spiritual, the vulgar and the symbolic, samsara and nirvana, the deeply felt understanding (that leads to nirvana) and its lack (that leads to samsara), and lastly good and evil.[63] In a sense, this appreciative acumen carries on the work begun by the first appreciative acumen that released and redeemed the experiencer's psychic energy, but then goes further by permeating the whole of a person's emotional, intellectual, and moral life.

Individuation needs a fourth appreciative acumen that leads from the person's "limited" wholeness, if we may say so, the experiencer's psycho-physical continuum set up by the three appreciative acumens we have discussed so far, to an "unlimited" wholeness that does not cling to anything and thus allows the experiencer to live to the fullest its nothing-ness/openness/fullness. This transition from the limited to the unlimited is effected by the fourth appreciative acumen, the "appreciative acumen that dispatches."[64] What it dispatches is the five gestalts complexity in which the (invisible) light had become visible, into the continuum of the whole's pure and primal symbolicalness.[65] In this way it completes what had begun with the second appreciative acumen.

The new pattern or *maṇḍala* that constitutes itself with the arrival of the four "insiders" and the revitalization of the center into a dynamic two-as-one reveals itself as a *process structure* whose structural aspect can be diagrammed as in Figure 1.2.

The unhorsing by the "insiders" and the central two-as-one marks the separation of the "spiritual" (misplaced into its travesty of soldiers) from the "instinctual" (the misunderstood spiritual represented by the horses) whose speed with which it panic-like races along, is figuratively, if not to say poetically, expressed by the "wind"[66] in its more tempestuous blowing. Since the instinctual cannot but have a hold on the spiritual of which it is its misplaced concreteness and which by the sheer momentum in it carries the spiritual away with it, the "severance," effected by the four intrinsically spiritual persons (under the guidance of the revitalized center, actively participating in this severance), can only mean that the instinctual is from now on unable to abduct the spir-

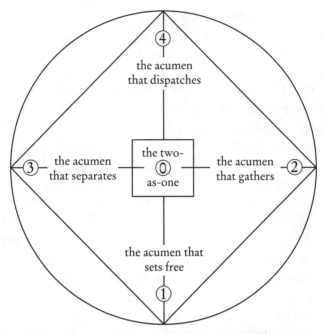

Figure 1.2. *The geometry of the interlocking spiritual forces.*

itual which now is restored to and stays with the original spirituality because, figuratively speaking, the wind has been taken out of the sails of the instinctual.

The culmination of this rescue operation is brought about by the two blood-related boys themselves who in their two-as-one capacity kill their jailers. It is of utmost importance to note that there is no word of either killing the soldiers and/or their horses—the rescue operation (vividly described from the outside) being, in Jungian terms, the individuation process (experienced from within) is not a suicidal affair. The killing concerns the experiencer's ego-logically determined dichotomy of the subject's "grasping and manipulating" that which "solicits this grasping and manipulating" and which the subject assumes to be an object before its gaze that has to be controlled. The killing of this dichotomy means that once the ego-logically imposed restrictions and restraints have been removed the light is *free* to shine.

Having regained their freedom, the two boys hurry away from the place of their confinement into a distant realm in which there is or, maybe, which itself is a castle that bears the name Nyi-ma-can. This name, which can be quite literally rendered as "being of the nature of the sun," intimates that this other, though not alien, realm or castle is not only one of brightest light, but also one of an intense spreading of light. As an archetypal image, the sun in a clear sky has been a favorite metaphor for the *lumen naturale*, the spontaneous thereness of wholeness in its more "pronounced" intensity.[67] In like manner, the sun is used as a metaphor for the experiencer's self-originated supraconscious ecstatic intensity[68] and for the experiencer's self-originated originary awareness modes,[69] the former indicative of a more "motionless" presence, the latter indicative of a more dynamic "functioning" that, by implication, sets up its own field character. Each originary awareness mode that because of its supraconsciously inspired cognitive quality is for ever active ("functioning") in instantiating an intensity-*field* that crystallizes into a gestalt quality according to the intensity that sets up and passes through these fore-structures of our existentiality, turns out to be, on closer inspection, a vector function whose value or gestalt is a vector. This idea, expressed in the traditional formula of three[70] (or even four or five)[71] gestalts as existential programs, not only resolves the dilemma of the one and the many—the one is the many, and the many is the one—but also allows us to speak "feelingly" of four suns[72] of which three are "internal" pattern-initiating and pattern-conserving field-gestalts in-form-ing their "external" configurations in such a manner that they seem to *con*-spire to build up the third vector-like gestalt to break out of the inner triarchic potential into an outer actuality that remains *in*-spired by the inner potential.[73] In this way the dilemma of the internal and the external that has haunted Eastern and Western thinking, is resolved.

The dynamics of this functioning is poetically expressed by an unknown author in two verse lines whose deeper significance will become clear as the story proceeds:

With the rays of the sun (as the) originary awareness
   (modes of) the supraconscious ecstatic intensity (that
   is the) king (himself, he)
Completely dispels the darkness (that is) the discursive
   thinking of the sentient beings intellect.[74]

In their hurry to reach the "castle of the suns" (as we may
now, on the basis of the above analysis, render the name Nyi-
ma-can), the two boys who in their togetherness now present
a harmonious blend of the spiritual and the instinctual that in
its previous disharmony had brought about the disaster that
overtook both boys, have to follow a certain way that must be
seen and known. But this seeing-through-knowing or know-
ing-through-seeing is not the ordinary ego-logically narrowed perception of something one desires to control and to
manipulate, it is an anticipatory envisioning, a creatively illumining seeing beyond the ordinary person's instinctual-affective scope of vision. This illumining seeing is, as a gloss to the
text explains, "effected" by an originary awareness, bright as
the sun, entering the seer's eye as two "lamps" whereby the
eye becomes not only a *visionary organ* but also the very *way*
to the "castle of the suns" set up as its terminal by the eye
itself, reminiscent of Johann Wolfgang von Goethe's dictum:

Ich wache ja! Oh lasst sie walten,
Die unvergleichlichen Gestalten,
Wie sie dorthin mein Auge schickt.
I am awake! Oh, let them reign,
the incomparable figures
sent there by my own eye.
             (*Faust*, "At the lower Peneios," part II: vs. 7271–7273)

and of his aphorism modelled after Plotinus:

Wär' nicht das Auge sonnenhaft,
Die Sonne könnt' es nie erblicken.
If the eye were not of the nature of the sun,
It would never be able to perceive the sun.[75]
             (*Zahme Xenien*)

From a dynamic perspective "lamp" means "flooding with light" and this meaning is implied by the coded names of the two lamps that make the boys see their way. The names are *dbyings rnam-par dag-pa'i sgron-ma* and *thig-le stong-pa'i sgron-ma*, respectively.[76] The first, the "field-purity-lamp" is, as is to be expected in this experiential context, not something static, but a process that because of its luminous and illumining, darkness-dispelling character, sets up its own "field" according to the intensity of the light pulsing in it, and also is "pure" in the sense that it is not sullied by restraints imposed on it by objectifiable properties that here, before they become such properties, retain their symbolical translucency. The "field" is therefore not some utter blankness, but an immaterial creative matrix that provides the material world with its non-material qualities. Inseparable from and, as it were, "inside" this field, is the second lamp, the "impulse-nothingness-lamp." The first term in its name is understood as meaning that it acts both in a particle-like and a wave-like manner simultaneously.[77] The second term "nothingness" intimates that it has nothing about it of substance and quality—categories of representational thought that obscure rather than illumine. In their togetherness these two lamps may be said to give an account of what may be said to be the *seeing* of seeing.

"Seeing" their way to their vision that like a beacon draws the two boys to it, they start "collecting taxes from the populace." The significance of this seemingly abrupt scene change from the luminous vision of a castle of suns to the harsh reality of ordinary life, is to make the reader or listener of this story guess the real status and nature of the two boys in their spiritual togetherness as the (once and future) king.[78] The clue to unravel what to all appearances is a mystery lies in the reference to the populace. It is one of three components in a social framework, the other two being the king and the minister, all of which are joined together in the sagacious maxim that declares: "By letting the king take his seat on the throne, and by putting the minister into prison, the populace will come to relax of its own."[79] All rDzogs-chen texts are unanimous in conceiving of the king as a symbol of the experiencer's supraconscious ecstatic intensity as it can only be known by the experiencer himself in a gestalt that impresses him by its meaningfulness; of the throne as the sky's immensity intimately "felt" by the experiencer within himself as the throbbing of the whole in the field that is his wholeness, and "perceived" outside himself as the clear sunlit sky;[80] of the minister as the ego-logical mind that by being put into jail is prevented from inciting the populace to disorderly actions; and of the populace as the five senses that, once they are no longer misguided by the selfish designs of the ego-logical mind, can relax and enjoy life. In the above story, a gloss explains the collection of taxes as a "gathering of the light into its original intensity."

With the real status of the two boys as being the (once and future) king brought to light, the story now proceeds explicitly on two levels, the "social," in the narrower sense of the word, "courtly" milieu and the "spiritual," the experiential expanse. The king is "counselled and conducted into an inner sanctum" by twenty-one court-ladies. Who are they? Why are there so many? And why is there this sudden change from an almost all-male setting into an overwhelmingly female setup?

Let us begin with answering the last question first since its answer will automatically answer the other two questions. It will be remembered that when the two blood-related boys who, in Jungian terms, presented the complementary relationship between the *persona* and the shadow, had been placed into a dungeon, the dark place of their own instinctual forces that paralyzed their spiritual life-force, they were firmly locked in it by an old and near-blind woman. This unflattering description reflects the identification of the two boys with their *persona* whose maleness is incompatible with anything female that consequently is suppressed and adds to the complexity of the shadow that now is male-female. The more the female aspect of the psyche is devaluated the stronger it grows and, as the story succinctly states, overwhelms the ego-logical male-oriented attitude. However, as an activation of the experiencer's inner life it also stimulates the process of individuation that, as we have seen, begins with the appearance of four "insiders" who combine in themselves what has traditionally been conceived of as being masculine in tone—the active, effective, rational, an Apollonian clarity that introduces and insists on distance—and what has been traditionally conceived of as being feminine in quality—the passive, appreciative, intuitive, a Dionysian abandonment that introduces proximity and paves the way toward intimacy with ourselves and all life surrounding and carrying us along.[81] In particular, with the "killing" of the restrictively narrow ego-logical perspective on life, a vista of brightest light and immense wealth and beauty is opened. In this transformative vision the "one" old, near-blind woman shows herself transfigured into "twenty-one" court-ladies who introduce and initiate the king into the richness of his inner life.

The twenty-one court-ladies who "counsel and lead the royal personage into the inner sanctum" that doubles as the throne room and the mysterious plane where wholeness in its unfathomableness becomes the wholeness that is our finitude,[82] are nuances of an intimacy that is quite different from any relationship between an "I" and a "not-I." The king's meeting with them is, as a gloss states, an "encounter" that, unlike a confrontation, is an empathic understanding of himself as what he is,[83] and therefore it is of decisive importance in any person's individuation process as the recovery and rediscovery of the lost wholeness in a new identity that is luminously *ek-static* through and through. From the perspective of wholeness these twenty-one encounters are the working *with* the light that we are and had "seen" in its symbolic image of a castle of suns. Working *with* the light means to "feel" it,[84] and to bring it into full play.[85]

The enigmatic number twenty-one sums up the various facets and nuances in the individuation process, each such facet or nuance being an intimate encounter with what we really are. What we really are is the coordinated hierarchy of three levels in a process structure in which each level has its own dynamics experienced as *its* gestalt[86] and, by implication, *its* luminosity, and *its* supraconscious intensity.

The first encounter is with the fore-structure of our existentiality, itself already the expression and the expressed of (the whole's) supraordinate and supraconscious intensity that, if we may say so, sets up its own evolutionary program informing the individuation process. Its structural aspect is our corporeal schema that is present in every experience of ourselves as being prospective embodied human beings and of our environing world as having human features, "meanings" that are already possible interpretations of it. As pure potential this (our) existential program is likened to a crystal[87] whose latent lucency under favorable conditions—the light of the sun falling on it—may burst forth in a fascinating display of colors. What this analogy[88] attempts to do is to facilitate our understanding of the enigma of human existence from a dynamic perspective. What has happened is that due to the whole's dynamics summed up in its ecstatic intensity that does not allow the whole to be "at rest for ever" and thus become a static One, a symmetry break has occurred: there is now an interiority and an exteriority, none of them being an absolute. The exteriority is a formulated luminous pattern of possibilities already prefigured in the unbroken potential of the original whole, but now experienced in what is called the "second encounter." A further symmetry break in this inwardly-outwardly experienced "exteriority" leads to the emergence of the whole's formulated energy as an individual's guiding image (toward wholeness) operating out of the luminous pattern of possibilities as its background.[89] Its experience is the so-called third encounter. Common to all these encounters is an intense luminosity.

Light[90] is the "stuff" we are made of and in our encounter with it we are re-living its dynamics within ourselves by becoming aware of it in its lighting-up out of the whole's pure and primal symbolicalness that in its "nothingness" is the Being-that-is-not and hence also its unorigination that in its lighting-up becomes its own energy, sending out multi-colored rays of light[91] that in us is our *lumen naturale*. In its opalescence it "colors" the whole's and our originary aware-ness modes that in their coloredness are creative, not passive, ways of seeing and knowing so much more so as they, each in its own way, set up a field that as the energy in them orga-nized in a special way is experienced as a gestalt.[92] Thus, in modern terms, light is not only its own wave of probability, but also a carrier wave of information,[93] and the information it carries is provided by the supraconscious ecstatic intensity that comes to us in images whose profundity and variety, self-portrayals of the whole's intensity, instill in the experi-encer a sense of the inexhaustibility of his very being.

In leading the king into the inner sanctum, the "bridal cham-ber" of the Gnostics,[94] the twenty-one court ladies undergo a further transformation and become the "queen"[95] whom the king holds dear as his very own illumining-inspiring intensity. As has been poetically stated by Śrīsiṃha:[96]

Just as a king does not allow any harm to befall
His realm and queen,
So a person who has received [his innermost mentor's][97]
    instruction
Will not allow the poison of concreteness
To enter his knowledge that the things and notions
    (constituting his outer and inner world) are (his)
    mentation.[98]

Now the scene shifts from the "spiritual inner dimension" to the "courtly external dimension." Five persons carrying shields or, according to another version, clothed in armor, station themselves at the door of the throne room and make it impossible for anyone to enter and, by implication, to leave. From the perspective of the psychic-spiritual dimension, the five persons are the five originary awareness modes that by the vigilance of the guards (their doubles) are protected from being contaminated by the instinctual-affective but also have no chance of "stepping out" and losing themselves in the divisive allurements of their own lighting-up.

The last two episodes in this story take place in the spiritual inner dimension. The first climaxes in the king's,[99] the supra-conscious ecstatic intensity's, self-cognition through its self-geometrization in the form of a *maṇḍala* or centered four that is both structure and function. Its functional aspect is symbolically presented by four persons looking into a mirror and recognizing themselves for what they are, the reflection of the central intensity whose integral functional aspect they are. This functional aspect, though unrecognized, they had already shown in the case of the two boys whom they helped in their struggle to free themselves. In Eastern thought the mirror is never a passive reflector, it is an active revealer and what it reveals is the true nature, as we would say, of what comes before it and is reflected in it. As the effulgence of the supraconscious ecstatic intensity it is the ground and reason for its functional lighting-up[100] that is always *its* function whose light tricks the ego-logical intellect into the belief that this light is something other than itself. The symbol of the mirror and the reflection in it thus acts as an invitation to the experiencer to "look deeper," to cognize and re-cognize him/herself for what he/she is and always has been.

The structural aspect is indicated by the reference to the throne room having eight doors of which only two can be said to be doors in a literal sense.[101] But even these are more like vector feeling-tones such that the one "door" felt as impure and therefore, in not being recognized for what it truly is and means, makes the experiencer (the ego-logical self) become involved with mistaken identifications and enter the murky world of samsara, while the other "door" felt as pure and recognized for what it truly is and means, makes the experiencer (the individuated self) "see" and firmly install himself in what is his/her legitimate place that is nothing else or less than his/her authentic freedom.[102] This realization is felt like a child having become reunited with its mother.[103]

The remaining six "doors" are the six "as if" experiential presencings[104] of which three are readily recognizable as ontological closures or modulations of the triune dynamics of wholeness, even if their listed order does not correspond to the order in which the intensities of the whole are discussed. This may well be due to the emphasis the experiencer places on the one or other of these "as-if"s in his experiencing them. There is thus the whole/"I"'s experience of what seems to be the whole's suprasensible light[105] that now in the five colors of a rainbow[106] engulfs the whole world; then there is what seems to be a presence of countless "divine" figures[107] or a presence of clusters of five resonance domains[108] with their respective gestalts who, imaged as royal couples in intimate embrace, are pattern-initiating and pattern-conserving fields with which the concrete individual constantly communicates and interacts; there is what seems to be the presence of the whole's originary awareness,[109] operating in modes that are intertwined with the resonance domains as the fields of their visionary knowing them—knowing is not a passive receptivity, but an active transformation and transfiguration —in and through the colors, befitting the domains and their cognitions, the whole's suprasensible light has assumed.[110]

The other three "as-if" experienceable presencings are the vectorial feeling-tones in the above experiences. There is a sense of non-duality,[111] of being in a "state" that is as yet unruptured by what makes up our prevailing rigid, narrow, and restrictive view of "reality" that makes us oblivious to the ecstasy and radiance of what we really are in our wholeness; then there is a sense of the limitations that hem us in, dissipating,[112] resulting, if we may say so, in the deeply felt understanding of the creative dynamics of wholeness, the *thinking* of thinking, in its closure of its whole/"I," to dissolve and dissipate into an utter insubstantiality,[113] and finally there is a sense of the whole's resonance reaching out to all sentient beings in tenderness/gentleness.[114]

The significance of the emphasis on the "as-if" in the above primarily visionary experiences lies in the fact that this "as-if" not only challenges the validity of ordinary perception, but also initiates an extraordinary intensification of the experiencer's sensibilities and sensitivities that invite and prompt the beholder to follow these visions *up to* their source, the whole's creativity or intelligence/spirituality. There is still one other aspect to this "as-if" that the fundamentalist, trapped in the cage of his/her unimaginative mind, cannot and will not see. This is its serving as an emancipatory device, designed, as it were, by the intelligence/spirituality itself, as a reminder to itself that in its lighting-up as its first step in its coming-to-know-itself, it already faces the risk of failure. After all, the whole's lighting-up comes with two "doors," indicative of possible avenues its intensity may venture up. The one, once the whole's light that is as much *its* light as it is our *lumen naturale*, has chosen and passed through it, will close behind us and hold us prisoners and will continue dragging us down into ever darker dungeons; the other will open wider and wider and let us re-discover the heights of the ecstasy of being out of whose serene intensity we may look at the world, which has lost nothing of its enchantment, without falling under its spell.

Certainly, as the story tells us, self-cognition as an experience of having come into our own is an occasion to burst spontaneously into joyous, jubilant laughter.

Notes

1. Ernst Kamnitzer, ed., *Novalis Sämtliche Werke*, vol. 3, fragment no. 271.

2. *Werke*, vol. 4, fragment no. 1745.

3. Strictly speaking, this term is highly contentious and reflects an unwarranted overevaluation of an ego-logical consciousness. For a critique on strictly phenomenological grounds, see David Michael Levin, *The Opening of Vision*, pp. 201f.

4. This version is found in the thirty-ninth chapter of the *Rig-pa rang-shar*. Its title, traditionally put at the end of the chapter, is *'khrul-tshul dang 'khrul-pa bzlog-pa'i le'u* "the chapter of an individual's tendency of going astray and his reversing this trend."

5. This version is found in the second volume of the *rDzogs-pa-chen-po dGongs-pa zang-thal* " re-discovered" by rGod-kyi ldem-'phru-can (1327–1386). Its title is *Kun-tu bzang-po'i dgongs-pa zang-thal-las rDzogs-pa-chen-po sems dang rig-pa dbye-ba'i rgyud* "The treatise on the difference between *sems* (mentation) and *rig-pa* (the supraconscious ecstatic intensity) according to the rDzogs-chen interpretation excerpted from the *Kun-tu bzang-po'i dgongs-pa zang-thal* ("Kun-tu bzang-po's spirited Design)." The difference in the two titles of this story deserves notice. The one, given in the *Rig-pa rang-shar*, preserves the "experiential" character of this story; the other, given in the *dGongs-pa zang-thal*, reveals a growing rationalization trend.

6. This is done by the formula *zer-te ya-cha*, which stands at the end of each paragraph or episode in the story and which itself can only be paraphrased in a lengthy phrase: "thus and so on it has been reported, and isn't that something wonderful!" At the same time this formula is an invitation to use one's imagination.

7. He is addressed and referred to by the term *"bcom-ldan-'das,"* being the Tibetan hermeneutical interpretation of the Sanskrit word *bhagavān*, usually rendered in English as "The Exalted One." The Tibetan translation-interpretation brings out the psychological implications and the non-reductionist experience of wholeness. According to *Bi-ma snying-thig*, vol. 1, p. 99, *bcom* means to have overcome the five "emotions" that as instinctual forces dim the luminous character of the five "resonance domains" (*rigs*), pattern-conserving and pattern-initiating fields, experienced as having a gestalt character (*sku*) and imaged in male-female figures, through which the experiencer senses himself as a "spiritual" whole (*ldan*). In this experience, he goes beyond (*'das*) the egologically reductionist belief that there are only three gestalts as postulated by the structure-oriented tradition.

8. They are individually known as *ḍākinī* in Sanskrit texts. This term is an adaptation of a vernacular term, *ḍāka* meaning *jñāna* intimating an originary, that is, intuitive and inspiring awareness (*ye-shes*). The Tibetan term *mkha'-'gro-ma* is a mechanical translation of the Sanskrit word *khecari* that has been hermeneutically interpreted in such a manner that *mkha'* is understood as referring to the sky-like openness of the whole over which these aspects of an originary awareness roam (*'gro*) in female guises (*ma*).

9. This Tibetan name is, once in a while, a literal and hence mechanical rendering of the Indian word Vaiśālī, the name of a country that has figured prominently in both Brahmanical (Puranic) and Buddhist writings, both in Sanskrit and Pali where its name is spelled Vessāli. This country,

named after its capital, was founded by its ruler Viśāla, who belonged to the Solar Dynasty going back to the Vedic period in Indian history.

10. This is his name as given in the *Rig-pa rang-shar*. It may be translated as "He who sends forth rays of light." In the version contained in the *dGongs-pa zang-thal*, his name is 'Od-'bar-ba, which may be translated as "Blazing Light." In both cases, the emphasis is on light. Mythologically speaking this tallies with the account of the ruler's lineage pertaining to the Solar Dynasty.

11. Brackets indicate the additions in the "smoother" version.

12. *ling-tog* is the name of an eye disease, ranging from cataract to amaurosis.

13. This name contains a direct reference to the sun (*nyi-ma*) and may be rendered as "of the nature of the sun."

14. This fivefold complexity is technically known as *phun-sum-tshogs* of which Klong-chen rab-'byams-pa has given a hermeneutical interpretation in his *Theg-mchog*, vol. 1, p. 221. The three other features in the fivefold complexity's transformations, remaining coordinated throughout the transformation process, have been detailed by Padmasambhava in his *Nyi-zla'i snying-po*, fol. 19a. They are (1) the fivefold complexity of the whole's pre- and proto-origination (*sngon-byung thog-ma'i phun-sum-tshogs*), (2) the fivefold complexity of the whole's self-originated creative dynamics (*rang-byung rtsal-gyi phun-sum-tshogs*), and (3) the fivefold complexity of the indivisibility of the whole (Being) and its creative dynamics (*gzhi rtsal dbyer-med phun-sum-tshogs*). Actually number 3 does not constitute a new (third) complexity, but merely points out that the complexities 1 and 2 are a unique process-structure that has been split for descriptive purposes. A real "third" complexity that can be counted as a fourth is the fivefold complexity of epigoni (*rjes-'jug phun-sum-tshogs*). It is on the first two levels, when viewed as a process evolving from its purely "virtual" state into its more "actual" state, that the teacher-entourage (teacher-disciple) relationship takes on a more "concrete" character. in mythologizing language, the process is depicted as archetypal man (*khye'u chung*), the larval stage of a person's individuation process, coming to the fore and asking the teacher; in experiential terms, this process is described as the experiencer's inherent intelligence/spirituality (*rang-rig*) stirring and then beginning to radiate in its own light and brilliance (*rang-gsal*). On the idea of "archetypal Man" (*khye'u chung*) see Introduction, p. 23 n.40.

15. Even the historical Buddha, the "one who has become spiritually awake," never spoke of himself as being something other than a teacher.

16. In his *Nam-mkha'i mtha' dang mnyam-pa*, fol. 287a, Padmasamb-hava speaks of "six" kingly teachers (*ston-pa'i rgyal-po*) of whom the first three constitute a pre-primordial triad or trinity (*ye-thog ye-gnas-kyi ston-pa gsum*) whose "spiritual emanations" (*thugs-kyi sprul-pa*) are Kun-tu bzang-po, rDo-rje sems-(dpa'), and dGa'-rab rdo-rje. The similarity (not identity) of Padmasambhava's idea, particularly as it relates to dGa'-rab rdo-rje (who was he after all?) with the Valentinian docetism in Gnos-ticism, is unmistakable The difference is that there is no savior figure in Buddhism; humankind has landed itself by itself in a mess out of which it has to extricate itself by itself.

17. From about the seventeenth century onward, this concept was sys-tematically excluded from the emergent rationalistic scientific outlook and was permitted to linger on as an anaemic figure of speech, the "natural light of reason." See, for instance, David Michael Levin, *The Opening of Vision*, pp. 447–453; Marie-Louise von Franz, *Individuation in Fairytales*, p. 169.

18. From the perspective of its actual experience in all its immediacy, the texts speak of it by its name of "self-awareness" (*rang-rig*) in terms its "self-originatedness" (*rang-byung*) and its being one's authentic Self (*rig-pa = bdag-nyid*) that is cognitively functioning in originary awareness modes (*ye-shes*). Thus, the *sPros-bral don-gsal*, fol. 7a states:

> Since it is beyond the reach of causes and conditions it is self-origi-nated (*rang-byung*). Since this ecstatic intensity (*rig-pa*) that has not come about in a random manner but has been present since time before time (*ye*), has become (the experiencer's) authentic Self (*bdag-nyid*), it is spoken of as originary awareness modes (*ye-shes*).

19. See above introduction, p. 14 and p. 32 n. 83.

20. *Nyi-zla'i snying-po*, fol.23b: *yul mkha'-klong kun-'byung yangs-pa-can-gyi pho-brang*. In his *Nyi-zla 'bar-ba* (sDe-dge ed., vol. 2, fols. 343a–351a), fol. 348b, Padmasambhava speaks of the "royal country that is of the vastness of Being's internal logic (*rgyal-yul chos-nyid yangs-pa-can*).

21. *sPros-bral don-gsal*, fol. 6b.

22. This paraphrase of the code term *gzhon-nu bum-pa('i) sku*, fre-quently found in rDzogs-chen texts, is based on the hermeneutical inter-pretation in Klong-chen rab–'byams-pa's *Zab–yang*, vol. 2, p.218, that itself is an emendation of Padmasambhava's version in his *sPros-bral don-gsal*, fol. 7b.

23. This idea of a gestalt (*sku*) being both the expression and the expressed is explicitly stated in the *Klong-gsal*, a work that has been lost except for numerous quotations from it in rDzogs-chen literature. In his

mKha'-'gro yang-thig [abbr.: *mKha'-yang*], vol. 2, p. 378, Klong-chen rab–'byams-pa adduces the following quotation from it: *rang-gi rig-rtsal sku-lngar shar*, which can be paraphrased as

> The creative dynamics of the whole's and, by implication, the individual's supraconscious ecstatic intensity presences itself in five gestalts (constituting the complexity of an individual's existentiality).

We must never forget that we as living beings—dynamic systems—are the whole and only part of it—"fractals" (endlessly repeated self-similarities). This modern concept "fractal" has already proved its usefulness in many areas and its extension to the old concept of *sku* is not at all a farfetched notion. It is a well-known fact that fractals are characterized by *self-similarity* in which a given figure or motif keeps repeating itself on an ever-diminishing scale. In rDzogs-chen thought, the motif is Being/wholeness that repeats itself in its gestalts (*sku*) that together form the geometrical figure of a centered four, known as a *maṇḍala*. Each of the five gestalt/fractals are anthropomorphically referred to by what seems to be a "proper name" that actually is what Ernst Cassirer called "symbolic pregnance"—a sense experience, a meaning, and the manner the former contains the latter. Without going into details these names/symbols are rNam-(par) snang-(mdzad), in Sanskrit Vairocana, Mi-bskyod rdo-rje (Akṣobhya-vajra), Rin-chen 'byung-ldan (Ratnasambhava), sNang-ba mtha'-yas (Amitābha), and Don-yod grub–pa (Amoghasiddhi). See for instance *mKha'-yang*, vol. 1, pp. 358f. Viewed as process structures the five *sku* divide into the traditional triad of *chos-sku*, the pre-thematic experience of Being's (life's) meaningfulness, *longs-sku*, the contextuality of experience with its welter of figures of symbolic pregnance, and *sprul-sku*, the guiding image(s) in an individual's sociocultural development, and their "ontological" and "pre-ontological" dynamics: the *mi-'gyur rdo-rje'i sku*, Being's invariance and adamantineness as the dynamic that underlies the emergence of the above mentioned triad, the *ngo-bo-nyid-kyi sku*, the probabilistic functioning of the former, and the *mngon-par byang-chub–kyi sku*, the transformation of pure potential into actuality. See *mKha'-yang*, vol. 2, pp. 431f.

24. *sPros-bral don-gsal*, fol. 71b; *Theg-mchog*, vol. 1, p. 299. For further details about this idea of a sheath see introduction, p. 30 n. 72.

25. *sPros-bral don-gsal*, fol. 71b. On this technical term that in rDzogs-chen (sNying-thig) literature has always been understood as a concept by intuition (not by postulation), see also introduction, p. 30 n. 72. The difference between *rin-po-che'i sbubs* and *chos-sku* is such that the former term emphasizes the "feeling" of being enfolded in a larger whole, while

the latter emphasizes the "visual" awareness of this larger whole as it dawns upon us when our vision has been released from the restrictions imposed by representational thinking that is so notoriously egocentric and logocentric. This experience of wholeness (not as some static entity but as a dynamic challenge) is filled with wonder and awe that carry with them a sense of mystery. Indeed, it is no exaggeration to say that we are "wrapped in mystery," as was long ago noted by Klong-chen rab–'byams-pa who speaks of a "sheath of mystery, the preciousness of Being's pure and primal symbolicalness (*ka-dag rin-po-che gsang-ba'i sbubs*). See *Theg-mchog*, vol. 2, p. 507; *Tshig-don*, 497. Another image, also conveying the idea of being enfolded, is a "precious box" (*rin-po-che'i ga'u*). See *Theg-mchog*, vol. 1, p. 297. In everyday life, a *ga'u* is a small silver box with an amulet in it worn suspended round the neck.

26. This change in diction reveals a trend in the direction of a more "rational" approach to what with Padmasambhava was still a highly *intuitive* experience. The outcome of this trend summed up in Klong-chen rab–'byams-pa's *mKha'-yang*, vol. 3, pp. 125 and 128–129, compares with the older experiential account as follows:

(Padmasambhava)	(Klong-chen rab–'byams-pa)
rin-chen sbubs	*lhun-grub rin-po-che'i sbubs*
'od-kyi sbubs	*ye-shes sgyu-ma'i sbubs*
bag-chags sbubs	*rnam-rtog bag-chags-kyi sbubs*

The terms *ye-shes sgyu-ma* and *rnam-rtog* in the right-hand column need a few words of explanation. We have already drawn attention to the fact that for the Buddhists the whole's possibilizing dynamics is an integral aspect of Being that in becoming its creative energy functions as its originary awareness mode(s) termed *"ye-shes."* It quite literally creates its own reference that in view of the fact that its creativity is a manifestation of Being's nothingness, its "is-not," is also nothing. This nothing-as-presence is termed *"sgyu-ma."* It certainly is not an illusion (which is a mistaken perception of something existent—a cairn mistaken as a person, for instance), and the Buddhists have always been careful not to be trapped into such a rash conclusion. The term *rnam-rtog* describes what we call "dichotomic thinking" and there exists between *rnam-rtog* and *bag-chags* (ingrained tendencies) a marked negative feedback link.

27. *gNas-lugs* III 4–5.

28. There is a play of words here: *'char-gzhi* "the ground and reason for there coming-into-being of what is called 'world'" and *'char-sgo* "the doors that open to what comes-into-being." These "doors" are our senses that far from being mere receptors actively mold what we call "world."

29. The "purity" of its pure and primal symbolicalness and the "opacity" of its world schema.

30. *bDud-rtsi bcud-thigs*, fol. 283b.

31. *sku-gsum*. The term *sku* is extremely difficult to assess because it refers to both the beginning of a process and its climax. There is nothing in the climax that was not already present in the beginning, though not in the manner of a mathematical equation. I have added the word "anthropic" in order to emphasize the rDzogs-chen thinkers' concern with the problem of growing into one's humanity (*Menschwerdung*) that is intricately intertwined with one's complex corporeal scheme or "body"-image (*sku*). Yet it is in this thrust of Being's (the whole's) anthropic drive with its wrapping itself around itself and forming itself into a "precious envelope" (*rin-po-che'i sbubs*), its "closure" as the *chos-sku*, that its closure-related limitations in its evolving field involvement, the *longs-sku*, become apparent, wherein the initially extremely faint "pre-geometry" of the live body scheme has to be worked out with the help of a guiding image, the *sprul-sku*.

32. These qualifications are meant to emphasize the fact that the teacher of our existential reality (as contrasted with our pseudo-reality played out in socially adaptive routines) is neither an ego-centric nor ego-logical hypostatization.

33. The almost inevitable use of numbers calls for caution. They certainly are not to be taken literally because the "one," the luminous teacher of the story who in his radiance sums up the complementarity of (the whole's) nothingness as the matrix of intensities (*stong*) and the spontaneous thereness of (this) nothingness in a brilliant light (*gsal*), is not a reductionist "One" that ever since the time of Plotinus has haunted Western thinking. So also the "two" boys are not literally two, but rather a new possibility of the original (father-mother) complementarity. Speaking of "two" reflects a change in emphasis focusing on the one pole or the other in the complementarity whose unitary character is tacitly recognized in that the two boys share the same fate. It is interesting to note that Klong-chen rab–'byams-pa in a gloss to the text interprets the two boys "onto-logically" as the whole's supraconscious ecstatic intensity (*rig-pa*) as functioning in the originary awareness modes (*ye-shes*) of the whole's pure and primal symbolicalness (*ka-dag*) and (its) spontaneous theresness (*lhun-grub*), which, as he explicates in *Theg-mchog*, vol. 1, p. 283, are indivisible (*dbyer-med*). A gloss in the version preserved by rGod-kyi ldem-'phru-can interprets the two boys "epistemologically" as *rig-pa*, an intense cognition, and *ma-rig-pa*, a cognition lacking intensity. If we were mechanically to equate *ma-rig-pa* with its Sanskrit equivalent *avidyā*, a

feminine noun, we would not have two boys but a brother-sister pair, which is contradicted by the opening statement of two blood-related boys (*bu-spun*). Klong-chen rab–'byams-pa's *ka-dag* and *lhun-grub* do not pose such a gender problem. A gloss in the text itself understands this puzzling expression to mean that after the light (that is the teacher) had split into *rig-pa* and *ma-rig-pa*, the (resulting) going astray is (the working of) *ma-rig-pa*. Since the Sanskrit equivalent of the Tibetan term *rig-pa* is *vit/vitti*, a feminine noun, there should be two girls and not two boys, which not only contradicts the explicit statement in the text of this duo being blood-related boys, but also shows that reading Tibetan texts through "Sanskrit eyes" can result in hilarious nonsense.

34. That they were mounted becomes clear later on in the text.

35. A good summary of the relationship between *persona* and *shadow* is given by Daryl Sharp, *C. G. Jung Lexicon*, pp. 97–99 and 123–125.

36. See introduction, p. 21 n. 30.

37. *Nam-mkha'i mtha' dang mnyam-pa*, fol. 289a

38. Ibid., fol. 289a.

39. It is worth noting that the idea of the Kun-tu bzang-po Kun-tu bzang-mo conjugal pair, playing an important role in Klong-chen rab–'byams-pa's writings, does not yet occur in Padmasmabhava's works. Wherever the idea of a conjugal pair (*yab–yum*) occurs with him, it is connected with the idea of a myriarch (*khri-rje*) at the head of the two higher levels in a tripartite division of the universe that owes more to gnostic speculation than to the Indian triadic cosmos. However, he is aware of Kun-tu bzang-po's relationship to the "pre-primordial spiritual wakefulness that is an invariant light whose quintessence is Kun-tu bzang-po" (*ye thog-ma'i sangs-rgyas 'od-mi-'gyur-ba'i rang-bzhin Kun-tu bzang-po*). See his *Nyi-zla 'bar-ba'i rgyud* (sDe-dge ed., vol. 2, fols. 343a–351a), fol. 343b. Otherwise Kun-tu bzang-po does not figure prominently except for answering the questions by rDo-rje sems-dpa'.

40. C. G. Jung, *The Archetypes and the Collective Unconscious*, p. 32. It is interesting to note that Jung connects this archetype with the anima, admittedly a controversial notion whose many misconceptions can be traced back to Plato's misogyny. Klong-chen rab–'byams-pa, *Theg-mchog*, vol. 1, p. 313, succinctly states that "appreciation" becomes and is the whole's "life force" (*srog*). "Appreciation" in which Kun-tu bzang-mo realizes herself and through which she expresses herself is "feminine/female."

41. The association of the cognitive capacity as "appreciation" (*shes-rab*), which always implies making distinctions between at least two facets or objectives, with the life-force (*srog*) that itself is associated with turbu-

lence (*rlung*) imaged as a racehorse, reflects a keen observation on the part of the experiencer. His/her life is as much instinctual as it is spiritual and each one aspect presents a possibility that might be followed up usually at the expense of the other. The instinctual is, in rDzogs-chen thought, tied to the individual's organismic-egological mentation (*sems*) riding, figuratively speaking, on a horse that as a symbol of the individual's vitality expresses the passions and other emotions with which he or she chases after the egologically predetermined objective. The image of the horse for the vitality in a person's organismic-egological mentation is used by Klong-chen rab–'byams-pa in his *Tshig-don*, p. 377. The image itself is already found in the Upanishads.

42. Like all concepts by intution, rather than by postulation, this technical term has many connotations according to context. Experientially speaking, *rlung* is felt as a current that, wind-like, passes through a network of force lines (*rtsa*) that themselves originate in the wake of this current. In connection with the life force (*srog*), it sets itself up as a field of bio-energetic forces (*srog-rlung*). See *mKha'-yang*, vol. 2, p. 99, vol. 3, pp 126, 187. As "turbulence" it is disruptive in the sense that the supraconscious ecstatic intensity pervasive of the whole is made to break out of its potential presence into an actual presence, technically spoken of as the whole's lighting-up (*gzhi-snang*). See for instance, *Tshig-don*, p. 178. Paradoxically speaking, the disruptiveness of turbulence is the whole's creative dynamics (*rtsal*) expressing itself in and through an originary awareness (*ye-shes*) that is pervasive of the whole. The intertwining of turbulence (*rlung*), originary awareness (*ye-shes*), and appreciation (*shes-rab*) has been explicated by Klong-chen rab–'byams-pa in his *Bla-ma yang-tig* [abbr.: *Bla-yang*], vol. 2, pp. 6f., as follows:

> The presence of turbulence in the dimension of (the whole's) supraconscious ecstatic intensity is such that as the fourfold life force it constitutes the stuff (the whole's) originary awareness is made of. That is, the central life force (that branches out into a fourfold) is there as appreciation (presenting the whole's) originary awareness as a function of its supraconscious ecstatic intensity. This (appreciation) may turn out to be the ground and reason for (an individual's) errancy (marked by) the emergence of discursive thought processes, or it may turn out to be the ground and reason (for an individual's) freeing himself, (a process climaxing in) self-cognition (as the re-cognition of his/her having been the whole's supraconscious ecstatic intensity, *rang-gi rig-pa*).

43. *mKha'-yang*, vol. 2, p. 126 clearly elaborates the connectedness of creativity with turbulence:

Thus, through the creative dynamics in the (whole's) originary awareness having come-to-presence out of the dimension of the (whole's) nothingness five (colored) luminosities originate; although (as such) they are the ceaselessly active supraconscious ecstatic intensity, there originates an egologically prompted "grasping" (*'dzin-pa*) of these five luminosities. This egologically prompted grasping is called turbulence (*rlung*). It is the outward movement of the creative dynamics in the spirituality (of the whole) as an inner luminosity.

44. In almost identical glosses this confusion is "explained" by the cryptical phrase *ma-bu 'dzol* "confused about who is the mother and who is the child." What is meant is that the "mother" is the *lumen naturale* that projects itself into enchanting images of itself, the "child," whom the experiencer takes to be his mother after whom he, like a child, runs. The elusiveness of this mother image leads the child ever deeper into the maze of samsara, which the child (the ordinary person) fails to recognize for what it is (*ma-rig-pa*). This chasing after a mirage is technically known as "errancy" (*'khrul*-pa).

45. Buddhist thinkers have been better psychologists than all the Western ones together. They distinguished between emotions-proper, which they termed "*kleśa*" (Tib. *nyon-mongs-pa*) "pollutants," and "catalysts" (*apramāṇa*, Tib. *tshad-med*), which included "love and friendship" (*maitrī*), "tender care" (*karuṇā*), "participatory joy" (*muditā*), and a "disinterested gaze/ equanimity" (*upekṣā*).

46. This hermeneutical translation is based on the detailed presentation of the five instinctual-affective forces in *Rig-pa rang-shar*, pp. 680–682. Each of these forces forms a set of five forces similar to the primary force. Arrogance, in particular, as a pollutant has been illustrated by five analogies that better than anything else bring out its unenviable features: in its domineering aspect, it is like a lion, in its paranoid vastness like the sky, in its ferociousness like a tiger, in its noisiness like a heron, and in its imperviousness like an elephant.

47. This triad of supraconscious ecstatc intensity (*rig-pa*), originary awareness modes (*ye-shes*), and appreciative acumen (*shes-rab*) mentioned in a gloss is again stated by Klong-chen rab–'byams-pa in *Bla-yang*, vol. 2, p. 7. The rendering of the last cryptic statement, *mkha'-la 'khyil-ba*, attempts to convey its intrinsic meaning. Mechanically rendered, the term *mkha'*, short for *nam-mkha'*, means "sky," but experientially it denotes that which makes something "tick" (*gnad*). As Klong-chen rab–'byams-pa points out in his *Tshig-don*, p. 281, that which makes an object tick (*yul-gyi gnad*) is *nam-mkha'*. As we would say, appreciation is concerned with the "immaterial" in the material.

48. The term *ling-tog* applies to any of the three kinds of an eye disease, cataract, glaucoma, and amaurosis. See also note 12. I have chosen the last kind in the rendering of this term in order to emphasize the near-blindness of this old woman.

49. *Tshig-don*, p. 188.

50. Here a word of caution may be necessary. The "not quite" (*ma*) does not mean that when *ma-rig-pa* is eventually resolved into *rig-pa* it loses it female character and becomes male. The Tibetan language is less gender-bound than the Sanskrit language, and from the mere look of these two terms they might be masculine nouns. However, it should be noted that in Sanskrit *vit/vitti/vidyā* (Tib. *rig-pa*) and *avidyā* (Tib. *ma-rig-pa*) are feminine nouns. From a psychological perspective that in the concrete human individual who combines both male and female traits, the intuitive-appreciative (*prajñā, shes-rab*) is assessed as feminine, the operational (*upāya, thabs*) as masculine. Hence, in the resolution of *ma-rig-pa* into *rig-pa* no change of gender or sex is involved. Nonetheless the patriarchal notion of "becoming male," figuring predominantly in Christianity (see Margaret R. Miles, *Carnal Knowing*, chapter 2) and reinforced by Greek-Roman misogyny, seeped into Buddhism *via* the *Sukhāvatisūtra*, the basic text of the Pure Land School that is still flourishing in Japan.

51. *rig-pa'i rtsal*. See *Tshig-don*, p. 376.

52. On this idea of a non-additive centered four as distinct from the additive pentagon with special reference to the Western context see Marie-Louise von Franz, *Number and Time*, pp. 120f.

53. The two "blood-related boys" illustrate the principle of complementarity basic to rDzogs-chen thought. As such they are a "two-in-one." The point to note here is that the two are both boys, not, as might be expected on the basis of the principle of complementarity, a brother-sister pair. The complementarity of the brother-sister pair is a common theme in Western fairytales and is heavily biased against the sister who acts destructively against her brother and only when she has nearly killed him saves his life. See Marie-Louise von Franz, *Individuation in Fairytales*, p. 24.

54. The center is the supraconscious ecstatic intensity (*rig-pa*) of which the *Rig-pa rang-shar*, pp. 555f. declares: "The intensity-"stuff" of the supraconscious ecstatic intensity (*rig-pa'i ngo-bo*) consists of a fourfold of appreciative acumens (*shes-rab rnam-pa bzhi*)."

55. *sgrol-byed-kyi shes-rab*. Grammatically speaking, this "appreciative acumen" (*shes-rab*) is a feminine noun and what it stands for has been

traditionally and iconographically conceived of as female. The same applies to the remaining three "acumens": the *sdud-byed-kyi shes-rab*, the *'byed-byed-kyi shes-rab*, and the *skyod-byed-kyi shes-rab*. Here, however, they have been functionally understood as so many aspects of the effectiveness principle (*thabs*) that, grammatically speaking, is a masculine noun and what it stands for has traditionally been conceived of as male. The situation depicted here makes any simple, reductionist explanation difficult, if not to say, impossible.

56. *Rig-pa rang-shar*, p. 555.

57. In his *mKha'-'gro snying-tig* [abbr.: *mKha'-snying*], vol. 2, p. 54, Klong-chen rab-'byams-pa explicitly states: "Any emotion is a presence of (the whole's) originary awareness in the concrete" (*nyon-mongs gang skyes ye-shes dngos-kyi snang-ba yin-no*).

58. *sdud-byed kyi shes-rab*.

59. *Rig-pa rang-shar*, p. 556. These two aspects of the fundamental forces, named after their effects—sky/space, water, earth, fire, wind, and referred to by the terms "*dvangs-ma*" and "*snyigs-ma*," respectively— intertwine in different degrees of "density." See *Zab–yang*, vol. 2, p. 254. A consequence of this idea, still rather disturbing for a Western mind, is the recognition of the fact that a person's psychic aspect is as much a biological phenomenon as is his/her physical aspect.

60. In *Zab–yang*, vol. 1, pp. 289 and 294, in particular, Klong-chen rab-'byams-pa explicitly states that this light (*'od*) has no color (*kha-dog med*).

61. On this important distinction, see David Michael Levin, *The Opening of Vision*, pp. 460f.

62. *'byed-byed-kyi shes-rab*.

63. *Rig-pa rang-shar*, p. 556.

64. *skyod-byed-kyi shes-rab*.

65. *Rig-pa rang-shar*, p. 556. There is no consensus about what is meant by five gestalts (*sku*) that emerge at several phases and levels in the whole's unfolding. Each gestalt has its "frequency," its light (*'od*). Each and everyone is reabsorbed into the whole out of which they have emerged and out of which they will emerge again in a "new" light. In speaking of the"continuum of the whole's pure and primal symbolical-ness" (*ka-dag-gi dbyings*), two dynamic notions have been rolled into one: *ka-dag* descriptive of the whole's pure and primal symbolicalness that in its openness/nothingness (*stong-pa*) is its energy-"stuff" (*ngo-bo*),

and *lhun-grub* descriptive of the whole's spontaneous thereness that in having a field character is commensurate with the intensity of its "stuff." It is here in this two-in-one that everything is still mutable. In the indivisibility of the *ka-dag* and the *lhun-grub* lies the formal justification for the ultimate complementarity of the external (the whole's field-like continuum) and the internal (the whole's nothingness as our experiencing). As contrasted with the (traditional) five gestalts (*sku*) as the expression and the expressed of their respective originary awareness modes (*ye-shes*) and, in the way they are listed, creating the impression of a static pattern, there is another five gestalts and five originary awareness modes complexity that emphasizes the dynamics of the gestalts and their awareness modes *in the making*. According to the *rGyud thams-cad-kyi rtse-rgyal nam-mkha' 'bar-ba'i rgyud* (sDe-dge ed., vol. 1, fols. 89b–100b), an explanatory work on Padmasambhava's *sPros-bral don-gsal chen-po'i rgyud*, by a certain Great Yogi Śrī-Ratnavajra, these gestalts and awareness modes *in the making*, descriptive of the experiencing of their experience, are mentioned nowhere else than in Padmasambhava's *yang-ti* teaching of which the *Nyi-zla'i snying-po* is the main dissertation. See fols. 94b–95a.

66. This poetic-technical term intimates the whole's motility as a kind of turbulence that forces the whole's "inner" light (*mdangs*) to move "outward" (*gdangs*). This movement is sensed to be like a gentle breeze, in which case it is referred to as *ye-shes-kyi rlung* "the breeze-like movement of the whole's originary awareness" (*mKha'-snying*, vol. 2, pp. 50, 161; *mKha'-yang*, vol. 3, p. 138) or to be like a violent storm, in which case it is referred to as *las-kyi rlung* "the storm-like movement of karmic blundering" (*mKha'-snying*, vol. 2, p. 50; *mKha'-yang*, vol. 2, p. 154f.).

67. In rDzogs-chen thought wholeness is never something static; rather, it has always been conceived of as a dynamic web of relationships that are consistent with each other and in their overall consistency "determine" what is meant by wholeness. Being nowhere and yet everywhere, it can at best be made intelligible by aesthetically moving and emotionally satisfying images. Such images are the sky, the sun, a crystal, a cloud heavy with rain, and a peacock's egg, the latter because of its opalescence particularly suited to illustrate the whole's pure and primal symbolicalness, its nothingness/intensity-"stuff" (*ngo-bo ka-dag*), an originary awareness mode that, as it were, "contains" within itself the whole's two other mutually consistent originary awareness modes, radiating from out of the whole's depth (*gting-gsal*) and ready to burst forth in playful activity (*rol-pa*), respectively. The sun, as has already been noted, illustrates in particular the whole's spontaneous thereness as its more "tangible" ownmostness (*rang-bzhin*), visibly experienced as the *lumen naturale*. The cloud heavy with rain illustrates the whole's resonance with itself and everything else as its region of concern

(*thugs-rje*) that in its (the whole's) creativity (*rtsal*) pours down like rain out of a cloud that has risen in the sky (*nam-mkha'*) intimating the experiencer's (ontological) openness/nothingness in its supraconscious ecstatic intensity (*thugs-rje rig-stong nam-mkha'*). The crystal illustrates the dynamics of wholeness by multicolored rays of light bursting forth from it and becoming reabsorbed by it without the one being added to or subtracted from the other. See *Zab–yang*, vol. 2, pp. 209f. These and other images have been listed in the *sPros-bral don-gsal*, fol. 6b. In his *sNang-srid kha-sbyor*, fols. 219ab, Padmasambhava devotes a whole chapter to the analogies used in elucidating the experiencer's spiritual growth.

68. *gNas-lugs* I 38:

rang-byung rig-pa don-dam nyi-ma-la
In the (experiencer's) self-originated supraconscious ecstatic
   intensity, the really real sun.

69. *gNas-lugs* I 40:

rang-byung ye-shes khong-nas shar-ba dang
rgyu-'bras mtshan-mo'i mun-pa sangs-pa dang
dge-sdig sprin-tshogs gang-yang med-pa-na
chos-dbyings mkha'-la don-dam nyi-ma shar
When with the rising of the (experiencer's) self-originated originary
   awareness modes from deep within and
With the passing of the darkness of the night, the (mechanical)
   working of cause and effect
There is no longer any gathering of the clouds of good and evil
The really real sun has risen in the sky, the dimension of meanings.

70. The three are the *chos-sku*, *longs-sku*, and *sprul-sku*. See notes 21 and 29.

71. These are the three mentioned in the preceding note, "augmented" by the *ngo-bo-nyid-kyi sku* and the *bde-ba-chen-po'i sku*, respectively. But see also note 59.

72. *Zab–yang*, vol. 2, p. 172.

73. *Zab–yang*, vol. 2, p. 174.

74. *Seng-ge rtsal-rdzogs*, p. 391.

75. In his *Farbenlehre* (Theory of Colors), p. liii in the translation by Charles Lock Eastlake, he says:

   The eye owes its existence to light . . . [which] calls forth an organ
   that is akin to itself; so the eye is formed with reference to light so
   that the inner light may encounter the outer light.

76. A detailed account on the basis of older texts has been given by Klong-chen rab–'byams-pa in his *Tshig-don*, pp. 271f. and 266f., respectively. Later authors merely repeat what he had said. The following is a mere gist of his presentation.

77. These specifications taken from modern quantum theory come closest to their "definition" in rDzogs-chen texts as "invariant" (*thig 'gyur-ba yod-ma-yin*) and "omnipresent in (its) lighting-up as an object" (*le khyab–cing yul-la snang*). See, for instance, *Mu-tig phreng-ba*, p. 497.

78. A recurring theme is the king getting up from his throne and leaving his palace. While he roams the country and gets involved with some woman, his palace is ransacked. Finally he remembers his real status and returns to his palace and, seated on his throne, he restores order. This and related themes have been collected by Vimalamitra (belonging to a different transmission line in the evolution of rDzogs-chen thought) in the *Thig-le gsang-ba'i brda'i rgyud*, a text we have mentioned before. See introduction, p. 24 n. 43.

79. *sPros-bral don-gsal*, fol. 47b. As an outline to learn about the spiritual life's mystery (*gsang-ba*) it is one of the most frequently quoted statements.

80. In his *sNying-po bcud-spungs nam-mkha' klong-yangs-kyi rgyud* (sDe-dge ed., vol. 2, fols.335b–343a), Padmasambhava devotes a whole chapter (fols. 342a–342b) to a hermeneutical interpretation of the term *nam-mkha'* "sky."

81. This dual character is expressed by their "names" that, on the one hand, describe their outward-directed "activity" and, on the other hand, their inward-directed and inwardly felt intensification of an appreciative acumen.

82. It is variously called "*tsitta rin-po-che'i sbubs*" "the precious envelope (called) *tsitta* " (see, for instance, *mKha'-yang*, vol. 2, p. 378) or "*tsitta rin-po-che'i gzhal-yas*" "the precious palace (called) *tsitta* " (*mKha'-snying*, vol. 1, p.29). Although the term *tsitta* is the Tibetan transliteration of Sanskrit *citta*, its has little in common with what is meant by *citta* "mentation." Rather, *tsitta* is used to refer to the level of quietness where the individual's spirituality is poised. In mythological language, this level of quietness is the residence of the "calm" deiform forces (*zhi-ba*) of the psyche and "located" in one's heart. Complementary to this level of quietness with its inner glow (*mdangs*) is the level of unrest with its light shining outward (*gdangs*), termed "*dung-khang*," "located" in the brain, the residence of the "angry" deiform forces (*khro-bo*) of the psyche. See, or instance, *mKha'-yang*, vol. 2, p. 197.

83. *ngo-sprod*. This term is explained in *sPros-bral don-gsal*, fol. 40a as follows: "what some one is as such (*rang-ngo*) shows itself by itself, and in so doing is encountered (by the experiencer)." In other words, *ngo-sprod* describes self-reflexivity.

84. The Tibetan expression for this "feeling" is *nyams-su len-pa* "to take to heart," where "heart" involves all the subtleties laid bare in the penetrating study by Stephan Strasser, *Phenomenology of Feeling: An Essay on the Phenomena of the Heart*. The importance of *nyams* is highlighted by the compound *nyams-rtogs* that can be mechanically translated as "feeling and understanding," but which more precisely means an "understanding through feeling," as it has been expressed in the Western world by Goethe:

Wenn ihr's nicht fühlt, ihr werdet's nicht erjagen
If you don't feel it, you won't catch it.
(*Faust*, "Night," part I, v. 534)

85. This "bringing into full play" is technically known as *sgom-pa* (Skt. *bhāvanā*) and is quite different from *bsam-gtan* (Skt. *dhyāna*) that describes a process of concentration on something or other. By contrast, *sgom-pa* has much in common with what C. G. Jung called "active imagination." Meditation enthusiasts who rely on dubious secondary sources in their muddleheadedness fail to make this important distinction and lump both procedures together in what is evocatively referred to as "meditation." On the important distinction between *bsam-gtan* and *sgom-pa* see my *From Reductionism to Creativity*, pp. 67, 92.

86. These gestalts (*sku*) or fore-structures and pre-programs of our existential reality (see notes 23, 25, and 31) are the well-known *chos-sku, longs-sku*, and *sprul-sku*. They may be "encountered" (*ngo-sprod*) serially or in their totality, in which case "four encounters" (*ngo-sprod bzhi*) are spoken of. See *sPros-bral don-gsal*, fol. 34a. Each of the three encounters are existential experiences of ourselves mediated by the omnipresence of our body schema (*sku*) that "makes it possible for us to articulate the human body with respect to its ontological dimensionality: its inherence in the field of Being as a whole, and the destiny, or ideality, for which this inherence claims us" (David Michael Levin, *The Body's Recollection of Being*, p. 67). Each such encounter involves seven "nuances" or "phases," as detailed in the *Yang-gsang bla-na-med-pa rdzogs-pa-chen-po sangs-rgyas ngo-sprod-kyi bshad-rgyud* (in: *dGongs-pa zang-thal*, vol. 3, pp. 519–531). Three times seven is twenty-one. When the story speaks of these encounters as "court ladies," it subtly intimates that by their sheer number, suggestive of the *richness* of a person's psychic life, they complement the *poverty* of that person's ego-centric and ego-logical ("male"-only) thinking.

87. *sPros-bral don-gsal,* fol. 34b. Padmasambhava discusses the appropriateness of this analogy with respect to how this fore-structure of our existentiality (*chos-sku*) is to be understood. This image has become the standard analogy for the individual's spirituality (the supraconscious ecstatic intensity, *rig-pa*) that "creates" its own "program" or operational basis (the corporeal schema).

88. Padmasambhava lists four analogies as a means to facilitate one's understanding of a difficult problem. They are a mirror, a mask, a halo, and the sun. See his *sPros-bral don-gsal,* fol.34a.

89. Both the formulated luminous pattern of possibilities (*longs-sku*) and the evolving guiding image (*sprul-sku*) constitute what is termed *gzugs-sku* "a gestalt-(experience) having a distinct contour."

90. *'od/'od-gsal.* Although often used unterchangeably, there is a profound difference between *'od* and *'od-gsal.* The first term is indicative of what we would call some "proto-light" or "quantum level light"; the second term names "(light's) brilliance."

91. The terms *skye-med* "unorigination," "(Being's) birth-that-is-not" and *ka-dag* "pure and primal symbolicalness" occur in various combinations with such terms as *chos-sku, chos-nyid,* and *'od-gsal* in Padmasambhava's *Nyi-zla'i snying-po.* See, for instance, fols. 25a, 44a. On fol. 43a he makes the significant statement:

> Although in the energy (of Being's) unorigination (*skye-med snying-po*)
> Its creativity (expressing itself) in rays of light (*rtsal-zer*) may come-to-presence as (inviting) mistaken identifications,
> These are not (present as such) in Being and (hence like Being itself) are of symbolic pregnance (*ka-nas dag*).

In this context, it is important to remind ourselves of the fact that Padmasambhava writes out of the immediacy of experience where boundaries, if there are any, are still fluid, resulting in the disconcerting use of one term when, rationally approached, another term should have been used. Unlike later rDzogs-chen thinkers, who write from the perspective of a reflected-on experience, he does not subscribe to the dualism of a *ka-dag ngo-bo* "the "stuff" that is "Being's pure and primal symbolicalness," and a *lhun-grub rang-bzhin* "Being's *eigenstate* as its spontaneous presence." Klong-chen rab–'byams-pa tries to overcome this dualism by saying that *ka-dag* and *lhun-grub* are "inseparable," "indivisible" (*dbyer-med*). See his *Theg-mchog,* vol. 1, pp. 282f.

92. This is clearly stated by the phrase *sku dang ye-shes 'du-'bral med-pa,* occurring over and again in rDzogs-chen(sNying-thig) texts: "a

gestalt and an originary awareness (mode) are not items that can be additively summed up nor subtractively separated."

93. On this character of light, see Fred Alan Wolf, *Star Wave*, p. 124.

94. For details, see Kurt Rudolph, *Gnosis*, pp. 245ff.

95. For want of a better expression, I have rendered *btsun-mo* as "queen." This term is not used to name "the wife of a king," which would be *"rgyal-mo."* Attention should also be drawn to the fact that the term *btsun-mo* was first used in connection with the twenty-one court ladies who appeared when the spiritual dimension had been opened up, hence *btsun-mo* indicates the "feminine principle in the nature of things," as we would say by way of concretization. She is thus the king's own femininity without whom he would, quite literally, be incomplete.

96. *Ye-shes gsang-ba sgron-me*, fol. 254a.

97. *bla-ma dam-pa.* This is Vairocana's explication of the *gdams-ngag* in the text. It differs from the *man-ngag* in the title in that the latter term intimates that the subject matter comes from "within" as an existential announcement, while the former term indicates that the listener conceives of this announcement as an "instruction" and an "injunction."

98. Lest the reader be misled into the misconception of this statement as professing some kind of mentalism (idealism), it may be pointed out that this statement is only the first in a set of five statements to guide the experiencer in his linking himself backward to his original/originary awareness. This "set" consists, as recorded by Klong-chen rab–'byams-pa in his *Zab–yang*, vol. 2, pp. 71f., of the following steps:

1. The assessment of what lights up (to become the phenomenal, *snang-ba*) to be mentation (*sems*),
2. The assessment of the dynamics in this mentation (*sems-nyid*) to be a (noumenal) openness/nothingness (*stong-pa*);
3. The assessment of the phenomenal and the noumenal (*snang-stong*) to be inseparable (*dbyer-med*);
4. The assessment of the many (*du-ma*) to be of one and the same flavor (*ro-gcig*); and
5. The assessment of the (experiencer's) originary awarenes (*ye-shes*) to be a continuous stream (*rgyun-chags*).

Special attention is to be paid to the distinction, common in rDzogs-chen (sNying-thig) works, between *sems* as a discontinuous event, the egological mind that from moment to moment identifies with any whim that captures it, and *ye-shes* as a continuous functioning of the whole's ecstatic intensity—there are no gaps in wholeness or intensity.

99. Strictly speaking, "king" is short for "the king and his consort." Both are complementary to each other, neither could be without the other.

100. Klong-chen rab–'byams-pa, *Chos-dbyings rin-po-che'i mdzod*, pp. 198f.

101. These doors are technically known as *"'char-sgo"* "the door through which wholeness dawns on the experiencer through originary awareness modes (*ye-shes*)," and *"'khrul-sgo"* "the door through which the experiencer embarks on mistaken identification through ego-logical and ego-centric mentation (*sems*)," See, for instance, *Nyi-zla'i snying-po*, fol. 21b, 30b; *bDud-rtsi bcud-thigs*, fol. 280a. This image of a throne room with two doors is reminiscent of the image of a mysterious cave with two openings near the city of Ithaca of which Homer speaks in the thirteenth book of his *Odyssey*. Porphyry, the Neoplatonist (233–305 C.E.), *On the Cave of the Nymphs*, has interpreted this cave as an image of the cosmos. Mortals descend into the cave through the gate of desire; the other gate, the gate of the gods, intimates the path of liberation, whereby the immortal part of the soul is set free.

102. *Bla-yang*, vol. 1, pp. 386, 389.

103. *Nam-mkha'i mtha' dang mnyam-pa*, fols. 300a, 309b.

104. *ltar-snang*.

105. *'od-ltar*.

106. Cp. Erich Neumann, *The Origins and History of Consciousness*, p. 323: "The unbearable white radiance of primordial light is broken up by the prism of consciousness into a multicolored rainbow of images and symbols."

107. *sku-ltar*, short for *lha'i sku-ltar*. The literal meaning of *lha*, from the viewpoint of its Sanskrit equivalent *deva*, is "a god," but in this context it is not an ontotheological term, but a phenomenological description of a felt enchantment by its luminous presence. This description and explication of the "as if" experience is the one given in *Bla-yang*, vol. 1, p. 386.

108. *rigs-lnga'i tshom-bu*. This is the description and explication of the "as-if" experience in *mKha'-yang*, vol. 2, p. 102. The highly technical term *rigs*, which I have rendered as "resonance domains," resembles, in its connotation, what Rupert Sheldrake, *A New Science of Life*, p. 72 et passim has called "morphogenetic fields" and Ervin Laszlo "psi-field" (In *International Synergy I S Journal*, 1987, pp. 13ff.). The "clusters" (*tshom-bu*) are endlessly repeated self-similar patterns—fractals in modern diction.

109. *ye-shes-ltar.*

110. The transformations and transfigurations effected through the originary awareness modes are technically referred to as *"sangs-rgyas-kyi zhing-khams."* On the exact meaning of *zhing-khams* see my *The Creative Vision,* p. 56.

111. *gnyis-med-ltar.*

112. *mtha'-grol-ltar.*

113. *zang-thal.* This term defies any analytical or intellectual definition. It "names" what can only be experienced and only inadequately put into words that are geared to the requirements of material life. The rendering of this term by "dissipating into an utter insubstantiality" attempts to convey something of the experience a person may have had at one time or another in his/her life and most often in what is reported as a near-death experience, when everything gross falls off and one walks right through a wall into what is called "infinity." To emphasize this "bareness" the term *zang-thal* is often used with *rjen-pa* "naked." This compound *zang-thal rjen-pa* is frequently used by Klong-chen rab-'byams-pa in his *Chos-dbyings rin-po-che'i mdzod.* Its use on p. 186 bears directly on the above passage. In his *sPros-bral don-gsal,* fols. 73b f. Padmasambhava explicates *zang-thal* as follows: "Since the manner in which the whole lights up has neither an exteriority nor an interiority it is said to be *zang-thal.*"

114. *snying-rje-ltar.* The traditional rendering of *snying-rje* by "compassion" is far from satisfactory, so much more so as it evokes images that are utterly alien to the Buddhist idea that stresses tenderness and gentleness on the part of the person who exercizes it. Literally the term means that the heart (*snying*) takes the lead (*rje*), as when we say that our heart goes out to someone. Similarly, its Sanskrit equivalent *karuṇā* stresses a person's concerned or caring action. The word *karuṇā* is derived from the same root *kṛ* as the word *karman* (Anglicized karma with or without capital letter). While *karman* aptly describes our careless and often utterly irresponsible blundering through life, *karuṇā* carries with it a numinous quality, intimated by the *u*-element in it. A person who exercizes *karuṇā* assumes responsibility for everything he/she does. Its highest expression is tenderness and/or gentleness.

TWO

Descent and Ascent

Our second story, too, reflects a world of supernatural light and its primordial experience that draws the visionary ever deeper into the immensity of his/its being by way of symbols as its best possible expression.[1] The story is told in response to the request of a group of ḍākinīs[2] who are specified as being white in color. This specification is not without significance. Not only is white the color of purity and purification, it also is in Buddhist thought associated with the fundamental force that is named "water" after its observable effect. Water is the liquid counterpart of light that transforms itself into the manifest world as a reflection of this primordial light and in so becoming reflected also "washes way" all the stains that as colored shapes may mar its pure gestalt quality appreciable by the experiencer's eyes that have been made to *see* rather than continuing to be merely receptive. The story, in many respects as abrupt as the previous one, runs as follows:

In the country named 'Khor-yug chen-mo,[3] in a huge swamp, an undying flame was burning.[4]

From [his residence called] mDangs-dang-ldan-pa,[5] it was spotted by the teacher Me-long-can,[6] who said:

"Well, you people of mDangs-dang-ldan-pa, I will tell you something. Listen attentively:

On the summit of towering Mt. Malaya,[7] in the lake Mu-khyud-can,[8] "Father"[9] 'Od-srungs[10] had sex with "Mother" rDo-rje phag-mo[11] and begat two children (a boy and a girl).

81

The two parents told their children:

"Son, go and retrieve the fire from the country of the Black Demon;[12] daughter, go and gather flowers from the rNam-par rgyal-ba palace of the ruler of the thirty-three gods."[13]

To these words the son responded by saying: "I am not going."

The two parents exclaimed: "What does this mean, you won't go?"

The son replied: "In the Demon's country there lives Halika nag-po.[14] He is going to imprison me."

The two parents again said: "Son, do not say so; in this country of the Demon there lives old woman Ling-tog-can.[15] She is your grandmother. Ask her for the fire."

The son said: "Well, honorable father and mother. This is not my territory; and yet you ask me to go there! [At least] send with me five servants, each carrying a beribboned sword tempered in sesame oil and a mirror."

The two parents were happy and said: "So be it." They got five men together whom they provided with swords and mirrors.

The son again asked: "Well, honorable father and mother, if I cannot get out of the Demon's country, what am I to do?"

The two parents answered: "In the country of Rin-po-che'i phung-po[16] there live four outcasts. Call them up to form your army. One will muster an army; another will loosen the shackles; and two will smash the (prison) door (for good)."

Thus, the two parents foretold.

With the words: "So I shall do," the son went away.

Now the demon Halika nag-po saw them (and exclaimed): "Ha, human beings on whom we will take our revenge have arrived!" He told his attendants: "Take these people and don't let them go." Five (from among his) attendants grabbed (the youth and his companions).

Old woman Ling-tog-can put [the legs of the prisoners] into irons and told the attendants: "These people have formerly killed my children. Don't let them go."

The attendants said: "We will do so," and so there was no chance (for the prisoners) to escape.

Then the youth said: "Well, grandmother, my parents told me: 'your grandmother lives in the Demon's country, ask her for the fire.' (So) do not hold me (prisoner), let me go." But the old woman replied: "I am not letting you go. Your father has killed my children. Therefore, I shall not let you go."

Then the youth said: "If you do not let me go I'll raise an army."

The old woman retorted: " Raise an army, I'm not letting you go."

Then the youth handed a letter to three visitors whom he told: "Well friends, in the country Rin-chen spungs-pa there live four outcasts. Go there (and tell them that) their perceptive youngster is held prisoner (in the country of the Black Demon).[17] Quickly send a huge army to relieve him."

With the words: "We will do so," the visitors left.

Then, for three days, every morning just when the sun had risen, many soldiers arrived, smashed the (prison) door, unfettered the prisoners, and banished the grandmother.

Five riders were unhorsed, and the grandmother's children were imprisoned. The (Demon's) attendants were decapitated.

Then the youth ran to his (home) country.

Arriving there he met his sister who had gathered many flowers from the palace of the ruler of the thirty-three gods.

The two parents were overjoyed when they saw (their children) having become the (actual) light (they had been potentially) and they conferred titles on them. The son was given the title rDo-rje lu-gu-rgyud 'dren-pa[18] and the daughter was given the title Mu-khyud 'dzin.[19]

When the teacher Me-long-can saw brother and sister communing with each other he advised them:

"Well, noble children,[20] listen. In the country Ma-bkod-par snang-ba[21] there stands a stūpa, made of crystal with five tiers. On each side five persons have positioned themselves in the forefront and have placed four mirrors of purest silver at the circumference of the crystal stūpa. Look at this from the peak of Mt. Malaya and (then) enter its enclosure. Once inside, climb up to the top-landing of a jewelled staircase whilst holding in your hands (a bowl) filled with (what is) the environing world and the living organisms in it. There on top of the stūpa resides the teacher 'Od mi-'gyur-ba.[22] From his right foot a rope of light rays extends. Be not afraid of it, but hold on to it. He is the father of your very individuation. Rush up to him. Beyond and above him is a house made of crystal with eight doors.[23] In it resides your mother sNa-tshogs-su snang-ba.[24] Recognize her (as your mother). Still higher up there is a house made of many jewels. That is your home. Take up your residence there."

Thus being told by the teacher the young man Lu-gu-rgyud 'dren-pa said: "I shall do so," and to his sister he said: "Let us do what the teacher has told us."

Having mounted the rays of the sun as their horse, seated themselves on the rainbow as the saddle, tightened a string of pearls as the girth, and holding a crystal as a dagger in their hands, they rode over the sky's orb as their way into their precious home, encountering no hindrances. How wonderful!

Overture: The Setting

The above story starts with an impressive depiction of the "place" in which the events in the ensuing drama occur. This place is the universe in which we live, or in which we think and believe we live, and as such is already an artifact of our mind—a model as well as a myth whose interdependence and intermeshing lock us firmly in a vicious circle from which it becomes extremely difficult, though not impossible, to break free. Unlike Western thought that until recently was dominated by a static world view, the Buddhist conception of the universe was from its inception molded by psychological insights and hence was basically dynamic. This essentially experiential universe was envisioned as a spherical vortex winding itself around itself in an ascending, inward-directed, and increasingly self-referential, vertical direction or in a descending, outward-directed, and self-forgetful, horizontal direction. In this movement three planes of existing are formed. Each plane presents a "closure" that is complete in itself, but in its completeness and closure remains open to and stays co-ordinated with the other planes as aspects of wholeness that, if anything can be said about it, is the *ek-static* intensity of Be*ing*. The "lowest" plane in this vortex universe quite "concretely" encircles and walls us in—prison-like, and our state of being locked up in it is "felt" like sinking deeper and deeper into a swamp, which contaminates everything in it and weakens us in our entirety (consisting of body, speech, and mind) by its miasma. It is, in mentalistic-experiential terms, the domain of the instinctual-affective that puts strong reins on the psychic-spiritual in us, which in this murky and dismal environment yet shines as an "undying flame," however dim its light may have become. This ever-present light not only makes us luminous beings *in essence* but also makes us strive to realize and make visible this very light. Yet we constantly forget and fail to see the presence of this light because our vision has been blurred, not to say blinded, by the "wrapping of ingrained tendencies or archetypal dispositions of experiencing ourselves and our world"[25] that gets tighter and tighter and, in the end, permits only the operation of a reductively calculating rationality obsessed with dominance over and control of objects or things, be they our own or another's body and/or mind. And so we have to be reminded of the presence of this light. This reminder comes from the "teacher" whose residence is on the next higher plane in the vortex universe; a luminosity that rests in itself whilst tending to spread, and through this movement runs the risk of ending up in misplaced concreteness. The name of this teacher[26] "Being of the nature of a mirror" aptly symbolizes his character of mirroring the luminous energy of wholeness and of making it visible to others who are receptive to it because of the flame burning in them. In other words, the mirror-teacher, as a reflector and revealer, quite literally brings into focus the next higher and, within the framework of the experiencer's universe, near-ultimate level that approximates wholeness. Wholeness as such cannot be subsumed under or reduced to any of its approximations. It can only be presented symbolically by the ("static") complementarity of a mountain and a lake as the locale of the ("dynamic") complementarity of (humankind's) ancestral couple.

The first component of this ("static") complementarity, a towering mountain, has traditionally been associated with firmness, immutability and immobility and also is related to our body as it is experienced in the immediacy of its lived concreteness as the common center of multiple intentionalities that presents itself as a gestalt or dynamic structure to the "seeing" eye in its unimpeded vision.[27] Thus, rDo-rje-'chang chen-po, the symbolic expression of wholeness whose dynamics is felt in each and every aspect of ours, "speaks" of himself/itself metaphorically:[28]

> Since time before time I have resembled a mountain (that)
> Abides unmoving and unchanging throughout the three phases of time.

It is from the mountain's summit, corresponding to the experiencer's head as a comprehensive term for the heart as the seat of the supraconscious ecstatic intensity of wholeness reaching into the individual and the brain as the dimension of

the creativity of this intensity—together they express themselves functionally as originary awareness modes that the
experiencer is able to "see" with fresh eyes and in this seeing
also to understand the gestalt dynamics of wholeness. Thus:[29]

Just as from the summit of the highest mountain (in the
world) the low-lying realms are seen all at once, whilst the
summit is not seen from the valley, so from the perspective of wholeness that (presences as Being's) spontaneity
that since time before time has been a (self)-dissolving
process[30] the claims of the nine intellectual pursuits are
understood as (being so many) self-presentations (of
spontaneity's dynamics); the other pursuits simply do not
understand the meaning and purpose of this wholeness.[31]

In the context of the anthropo-cosmic setting with which
this story starts, the name of the towering mountain is of particular significance. It gives the events that follow an additional human-worldly interest. According to the esoteric
tradition, it was on Mt. Malaya, a mountain range in South
India, that the meaning and purpose of Being had been
expounded through symbols and gestures to persons of a
mystical bent[32] by either Kun-tu bzang-po himself or rDo-
rje sems-dpa',[33] the former being wholeness itself turned
mankind's "first" teacher, the latter being a symbol of the
experiencer's cognitively visionary fine-structure.[34]

The second component of the ("static") complementarity
is the lake. From the perspective of the observer, the mountain may be said to symbolize the vertical dimension of the
universe and the lake to symbolize its horizontal dimension.
However, from the perspective of the experiencer there is
more to what at first glance seems to be a topographical
description of the universe. We must not forget that for the
experiencer the universe is not so much a conceptual-repre-
sentational model, rather it is a realm of situational possibilities through which he moves. For him such phenomena as
mountains and lakes are primarily images of symbolic pregnance,[35] not reductively postulated "things," and, as such, are

a challenge to his ability to understand their meaning(s) in his endeavor to realize wholeness anticipated and envisioned through its symbols. We have already noted that the image of the mountain is associated with a sense of firmness and constancy—something that remains what it is and that in the ultimate sense is the whole's supraconscious ecstatic intensity, "congealed," as it were, into our body-as-lived—, but also with the sense of sight founded on and spread out over the body-as-lived[36]—not only is from the mountain's summit the world displayed before our eyes, but we also see the mountain itself towering and sky-reaching from its environing "field" that for subtle reasons in the present case is a lake. Together, the mountain and the lake suggest time and space "appearing" jointly with differentiating frequencies out of the intriguing equivalence of matter and energy such that the mountain is "intense" matter involving dynamic tendencies in the direction of "extensive" matter, the lake, that remains what it is—intensity.[37] This is what is obviously meant when rDo-rje-'chang chen-po is made to say:[38]

Since time before time I have resembled a lake (that)
Since time before time has been without (the ego's)
    perturbations (determining its) interpretations.[39]

To the extent that the mountain in its loftiness is associated with the opening and vastness of vision, the lake in its depth and mysterious sheen is associated with the cultivation of the vision in its splendor without the ego's interference with what is "seen." By way of illustration, Klong-chen rab-'byams-pa[40] speaks of the sparkling and shimmering beauty of the reflection of the stars in a calm lake from whose water[41] they cannot be abstracted. As sensuous and sensual water phantoms, they are luminous presencings, not manipulatable objects.[42] The cultivation of this visionary experience needs a different mode of seeing and knowing: one that is not assertive and reductively discursive, but is more primordial, pristine—an "originary awareness" that in all its nuances remains in touch with the felt sense of the visionary field as an extension of the body-as-lived. These nuances are like waves that surge in a lake and always remain parts of its water.[43] Their pervasiveness has been poetically stated in the following words:

> The originary awareness modes (as functions of the)
> supraconscious ecstatic intensity that can only be
> experienced by ourselves is present in our live body,
> Like oil in sesame seed;
> The live body's splendour and luster
> Is pervaded by the moisture of the originary awareness
> modes.[44]

This moisture is quite literally visible in the glistening of the eyes of a rapt listener; similarly, to say that someone cries with joy is not merely a figure of speech but a phenomenologically exact description of a deeply felt and realized experience.

The name of this lake, Mu-khyud-can, "being of the nature of a periphery" is slightly reminiscent of the mythical mountain range that in Indian Buddhist cosmology surrounded the central mountain Mt. Meru, which formed the axis of this universe of ours like a fence.[45] The periphery, however, is unbounded and of a supraordinate light,[46] which means that the lake's size, if we may say so, varies with the intensities coming to pass. Correspondingly, the profundity of the visionary experience depends on the size of the mountain and the lake—the higher the mountain and the larger the lake, the wider is the vision and the larger the scope of its cultivation. These archetypal images evoke in the experiencer in his finitude a sense of feeling at home in such a universe which may prepare him for the "intimate immensity"[47] of space whose sensually felt and sensuously envisioned presence is the sky[48] into which his spirituality, bird-like, may soar. So rDo-rje-'chang chen-po is made to say:[49]

> Since time before time I have resembled the sky—
> The sky in itself has nothing substantial about it—[50]
> No dark spot or cover can be located in it[51]

and

Since time before time I have resembled the *khyung-chen*[52] (that)
In one sweep does away with what curtails vision.[53]

In this (closed) universe of ours that has evolved out of the (open) intensity of wholeness, the complementary images of the mountain and the lake are descriptors of its "physical" state that itself would be unintelligible if it were not for the complementarity of its co-evolving "mental" state whose descriptors are "Father" 'Od-srungs and "Mother" rDo-rje phag-mo, the one emphasizing structure, the other emphasizing process. As the name of the "Father," the masculine principle in the nature of things, "Preserver of the Light" implies, He is the gestalt in which the supraconscious ecstatic intensity expresses itself. As a supraordinate light that does not offer any resistance to its accessibility in the immediacy of its experience, it is the luminosity of an originary awareness. In other words, He is a *process structure*.[54] Similarly, the name of the "Mother," the feminine principle in the nature of things, "Adamantine Sow" suggests the pervasive force of creativity,[55] in the narrower sense of the word, fertility.[56] As the possibilizing dynamics of wholeness that in the symbolizing and mythologizing language of rDzogs-chen thought is called either "rDo-rje Phag-mo" or "Kun-tu bzang-mo,"[57] She combines in herself both the whole's "operacy" or effectiveness principle manifesting itself in a supraordinate luminosity that structures itself into an anthropomorphically envisioned gestalt experienced as the whole's meaning, and the whole's "value cognition as an intensification of its cognitive capacity" that manifests itself as originary awareness (modes) of which the gestalt of life's meaning is both the expression and the expressed. The indissoluble unity of the masculine and the feminine is "felt" as an *ek-static* (non-local)[58] rapture and "imaged" as the sexual act[59] between father and mother as the symbolic expression of an unfolding energy that in its unfolding does not set the one against the other, but leads to a self-reflexive self-transcendence in a new complementarity—the

twins who at this stage of the story have as yet no names and
so are more like probability process structures of luminous
intensities.[60] Through them the twins will have to find, in an
actively seeing manner, *their* way of growing into wholeness
of which Johann Wolfgang von Goethe spoke as *Geeinte
Zwienatur* (twin natures blended).[61]

Andante con moto: The Descent

Urged on by their parents, the twins must go forth and perform certain tasks, some of which are of a distinctly perilous
nature. The boy must retrieve from the country of the Black
Demon—his very name "Black Demon" already intimates
his sinister character[62]—the fire that the teacher Me-long-can
had spotted as an undying flame in a huge swamp that now
reveals itself as this demon's domain. The girl must gather
flowers from the palace garden of the ruler of the Trāyastriṃśa gods. Both these "localities" are dimensions or levels
in an individual's enworlded existence—*das Äussre ist gleich-
sam nur ein verteiltes, übersetzte Innre, ein höheres Innre.*
From a Buddhist perspective, we might vary this dictum of
the poet Novalis by speaking of a *niedrigeres Innre* (a lower
internal) and reserve and associate, for purely descriptive-
analytical purposes, his *höheres Innre* (higher internal) for
and with the flame as a symbol of an individual's *lumen naturale*, his/her supraconscious ecstatic intensity in whose
unfoldment the "teacher," a guiding image of vital importance, plays a significant role, first by pointing out its presence as well as its source, involving an immanent tension, not
a dualistic opposition, expressed in the image of the "parents" engaged (or having engaged) in a sexual act, and later, as
the story develops, by speaking of the direction in which this
supraconscious ecstatic intensity is to move.

For the time being the story focuses on the boy's mission,
the retrieval of the light (flame), and the predicament in which
he will find himself and out of which he will emerge
unscathed.[63] The boy is fully aware of the danger of venturing

into this fearful territory whose ruler is certain to imprison him, if not, as his personal name "Black Halika" suggests, even to poison him, and he flatly refuses to go. His refusal shows that he is still far from possessing or presenting the supraconscious ecstatic intensity that is his true being and that he is still trapped in an ego-logical mode of seeing. So in order to make him relinquish his ego-centricity and feel some concern for others the two parents appeal to his "brighter," compassionate nature by telling him that in this baleful country under the rule of the Black Demon there lives an old woman whose plight is made worse by her being almost totally blind—"she who suffers from amaurosis"[64]—and that this old woman is his grandmother. Actually, this old woman is his "darker" side,[65] a state of diminished awareness and spiritual blindness whose presence he has to recognize if he is not to continue in the trap set by it which he was about to perpetuate by his ego-centricity. This "darker" side of his, the apparent lack of an ecstatic intensity (*ma-rig-pa*) is not so much an absence as a malfunctioning of this intensity as the whole's pervasive spirituality and resonance (*thugs-rje/rig-pa*). This malfunctioning is co-emergent with and complementary to its proper functioning in originary awareness modes (*ye-shes*) that likewise is co-emergent with and complementary to its malfunctioning.[66] This co-emergence is the primordial auto-manifestation of wholeness at the "moment" of its coming-to-presence as a risk-taking wholeness through the spirituality/resonance aspect in the triune dynamics of wholeness that forces it to cross its instability threshold. Although we may speak of this diminished intensity as the whole's time-bound consistency with itself and everything else that for all practical purposes is synonymous with the affective "state" of dullness, so characteristic of ordinary beings, *its* intensity produces another "deficiency intensity" that as an integral aspect of it has been with it since its very onset and that constitutes the solipsistic fallacy with its ego-centered transcendentalism. With the emergence of the ego, there occurs an inevitable fragmentation of the unity of experience. Each fragment can be labeled as this or that with the result that each such label assumes a life of its own and becomes a reality that leads us into the illusion that the mentioning of the label is the equivalent of the experience. This is termed the conceptual fallacy.[67]

The appeal to the boy's "brighter" side by his parents has the desired effect. He is willing to go. But he is still too much concerned about himself and wants to be accompanied on his journey into an alien country by five servants who are to look after his safety by carrying swords and mirrors. According to Buddhist thinking with its emphasis on the spiritual in a human being, the sword symbolizes a person's discriminative-appreciative acumen whose sharpness cuts asunder the instinctual-affective bonds. The mirror, as noted before, reflects and reveals the unfurling of the whole's supraconscious ecstatic intensity in the five translucent rainbow-like colors of originary awareness modes as its functions. A less astute person tends to mistake them as so many independent entities and then is trapped by them in realms of a mistaken and misplaced concreteness.[68] For this reason, he is in dire need of the sword of a discriminative-appreciative acumen with its ribbons symbolizing the rays of the whole's five-colored effulgence and thus establishing an intimate connectedness between the mirror and the sword.

Although the parents readily accede to his request, he is still caught up in his ego-centeredness. "What am I to do if I cannot get out of the Black Demon's realm?" The parents advise him to enlist the help of four "outcasts" in a country whose name is spelled differently in different versions,[69] each different spelling possibly reflecting on the scribe's understanding of the name's symbolic significance.[70] All of them imply that something precious and valuable is intended—"Pile of Valuables," as we may very prosaically translate its evocative Tibetan name. In any case, the very wording of the advice intimates that the boy's task is an intra-psychic adventure, a journey into a region shunned by ordinary people. The country's "preciousness" consists of the completeness of the dynamic qualities of wholeness. They are summed up in the experience that in its vastness has a "field"-

like character where meanings are born, inseparable from the field's "excitation," the supraconscious ecstatic intensity that prompts wholeness to be creative. Speaking of it as a "pile" points to the supercompleteness of inexhaustible originary awareness modes.[71] More intriguing is a gloss that explains this name as a palace-like area called *tsitta*,[72] somewhere in the region we call our "heart,"[73] the center and core of any living (human) being's experience. Conceived of and elaborated as a sheath or an envelope,[74] this "place" is the mystery of our being. From the perspective of wholeness it is not something over and above or anywhere (which would turn it into a meaningless postulate or, at best, into a quantifiable, measurable, and localizable entity). Rather, in its dynamics, wholeness (the "big" mystery, "the nothingness that is the same as fullness," of which C. G. Jung spoke)[75] wraps itself around itself and creates another, dough-nut-like, wholeness (a "little" mystery or nothingness-full-ness)—the "precious envelope"—that has lost nothing of its original wholeness and preciousness, but now is the "mystery" of our own being.[76] In other words, what has happened is that the pre-experienceable wholeness has become an experienceable wholeness in a gestalt, a dynamic energy pattern that, in the immediacy of its luminous presence, is the whole's meaning whose visibly felt experience is effected by an originary aware-ness mode.

Here it may not be out of place to point out the ambiguity that attaches to the use of the word "experience" in that it does not clearly distinguish between what in German is called *Erfahrung* und *Erlebnis*, respectively. Usually, we understand by experience an experience *of* that because of its strong per-ceptual character allows itself to be conceptualized and be turned into a perceptual judgment, which is precisely what is meant by *Erfahrung*. But there is also another kind of experi-ence that is intuitive-ecstatic and, rather than presenting a frag-mented or fragmentary "picture," yields a lived unity, spoken of in German as *Erlebnis*. The complexity of Being's triune dynamics, as understood in experience (*Erfahrung*) by Klong-chen rab-'byams-pa, can be diagrammed as in figure 2.1.

A. The pre-ontological triune process structure of Being already expressing the fundamental interdependence of structure and function

(a) The "structural" aspect of the structure-function interdependence

Being's intensity-"stuff" $\longleftrightarrow$ eigenstate $\longleftrightarrow$ spirituality-resonance[77]

symbolical   spontaneous   holistic

(b) The "functional" aspect of the structure-function interdependence

voidance $\longleftrightarrow$ radiance $\longleftrightarrow$ *ek-stasis*

B. The ontological triune process structure of Being as forming an individual's existentiality

fore-structure or anthropic gestalt $\longleftrightarrow$ [*lumen naturale*] $\longleftrightarrow$ originary awareness (modes)

Note: Here $\longleftrightarrow$ means "if, and only if, then"

Figure 2.1. *The pre-ontological and ontological process structures.*

With Padmasambhava the complexity of this triune process-structure of Being is more difficult to assess because of its self-referential character in the sense that we as experiencers *are* this Being and only part of it—"as a water molecule is the river and yet only part of it."[78] In terms of the experiencer, Being "relives" its own dynamics, not in separable details, but holistically on different levels. His starting point is Being, the "ground-that-is-not," and the "lighting-up" of this ground-that-is-not.[79] Each "level," if we may say so, presents a triune complexity can be diagrammed as in figure 2.2.

Returning to the mainstream of the story, the question is who are the four "outcasts" and how do they fit in? By referring to outcasts whose help the boy will have to enlist, the parents show how well they understand their son's psychology and gently censure his ego-centered attitude—"*I* am not going"; "if *I* cannot get out of the Demon's country what am *I* to do"—that is so characteristic of the rationalist's approach to reality, recognizing only his specific point of

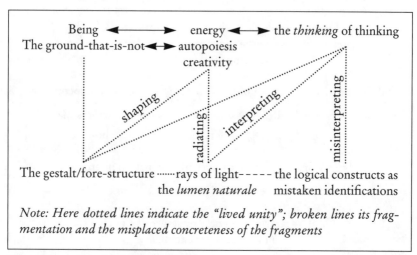

Note: Here dotted lines indicate the "lived unity"; broken lines its fragmentation and the misplaced concreteness of the fragments

Figure 2.2. *The Unfolding of Being.*

view and considering everything that does not fit into its narrowness as of no great relevance and consequently excluding it from his consciousness—"repressing" it, as the psychoanalysts say. The "outcasts" are the repressed or unrecognized facets and forces of the psyche. Securing their help begins with the recognition of their presence and is followed by the establishment of a relationship with them through intermediaries, as the story states at a later stage. As the unrecognized forces of the psyche the four outcasts are its "cognitive" and "illumining" functions, figuratively spoken of as "lamps."[80] In the individual's everyday context the cognitive function is his critical acumen,[81] but in this intra-psychic context it is to be understood as the "arousal" of the "psychic potential," itself the creative dynamics of the whole's supraconscious ecstatic intensity or of the whole's resonance with itself and everything else in its range.[82]

In detailing the steps taken by the four outcasts, who are so many exteriorized aspects of the psychic potential arousal, to help the boy in his imprisonment by the demonic forces of his having become enworlded, a close cooperation between two from among the four becomes strikingly evident. The story takes place on two levels, a worldly one and a psychic one.The sequence of the actions that are performed by each partner in each twosome is reversed in each of the two levels. On the concrete worldly level, the "mustering" of the army, the "gathering" of what there is[83] in the fateful subject-object split into the lighting and unity of an originary awareness,[84] occurs prior to the "loosing of the prisoner's shackles"; on the psychic level there takes place the "differentiating" between the phenomenal (the object phase) and its perceiving (the act phase of the cognitive process)[85] and between samsara and nirvana, the former being the lack of the deeply felt understanding of the *lumen naturale* and the latter being its deeply felt understanding.[86] Speaking of a "sequence," however, we must not allow ourselves to be led into the trap of the literalist's fallacy; the two arousals present an intertwining of processes, each presupposing and/or anticipating the other for its efficacy. I must have an idea of what I want to do ("loosing the shackles") so that I can gather the necessary forces ("mustering the army"), but I also must have mustered the forces in order to succeed in what I want to do. These same observations and remarks apply to the second pair of outcasts/arousals, listed separately only in a gloss that complicates matters.[87]

Thus assured that help is forthcoming, the son is ready to depart.

It will have been noted that so far nothing further has been said about the girl's visit to the rNam-par rgyal-ba (Skt. Vaijayanta) palace of the ruler of the Trāyastriṃśa gods where she is to collect flowers, and she does not appear again until after her brother's quest and, by implication, her own mission have been completed and so that the two can jointly hurry home. Nonetheless a highly dramatic and spectacular contrast between their destinations is pictured. While the brother descends from the bright supramundane world of his parents into the darkest realm of fearsome demons, the sister, too, descends, but only into the lucent world of the gods whose residence is on the summit of Mt. Meru, the mythic axis of our world system, which is not too far from the shining supramundane world she had to leave for a while. The name of the palace itself is very significant. It means "victory over whatever is not conducive to the realization of Self-hood." There is a *double entendre* in the flower (or flowers)[88] she is to bring home. We have already noted that the story moves on two levels. Accordingly, on the concrete worldy level, the girl is to grow into a woman whose first visible sign is the onset of the menstrual cycle.[89] On the psychic level her inner potential is to mature into the whole system's originary awareness mode as a function of its supraconscious ecstatic intensity symbolized by a flower:

> The flower that is the supraconscious ecstatic
>   intensity's originary awareness
> Is hidden under the root system of the emotions (with)
>   the drop in ecstatic intensity (in the lead).[90]

But potentially a flower also contains its fruit:

> In the flower, the originary awareness (as a shining)
>   lamp,
> The fruit, the triune gestalt pattern (of wholeness), is
>   completely (prefigured).[91]

The implication is that in a certain sense the sister (the feminine principle) is, poetically speaking, the flower that, unpoetically speaking, is pure potential and as such cannot but unfold and "create" (itself into) a patterned field of exquisite beauty, each creative phase being an ornament to itself and the whole.[92]

In spite of the deceptively easy differentiation between brother and sister and their individual psychologies, the story depicts a situation that complicates the issue. Since we in the West under the impact of Plato's and, in particular, Aristotle's misogyny tend to associate creativity with the masculine principle in nature (whatever that may mean), it comes somewhat as a surprise that the sister has such masculine traits, while the brother, who somehow presents the psychic potential arousal, traditionally contrasted as the feminine appreciative acumen with the masculine effectiveness principle, has distinct feminine traits. All this shows that simple, rational-reductive approaches and gender-related conclusions are out of place in connection with rDzogs-chen process thinking.

Allegro vivace: Captivity and Rescue

Soon after the youth had left his parents' luminous realm and crossed into the land of the demons, he and his companions were spotted by the demon Halika nag-po ("black aconite") who at once ordered the ruffians of his retinue to capture them whom he, true to his character, venomously and vindictively brands as "human beings on whom he will take his revenge." As the "dark" side of the psyche, this demon presents and sums up the primarily instinctual forces that consider any intrusion by the "bright" side of the psyche, the spiritual, as a threat that has to be dealt with immediately. Interestingly what this black demon feels about the shining youth is the same as what the youth felt about the demon when he was still with his parents and refused to go. Each sees a potential threat to himself in the other. From the demon's point of view the best thing to counter this threat is to capture the intruders and to put them into prison—psychologically speaking, to repress what they stand for. To make sure that an escape is impossible an old near-blind woman called "Ling-tog-can" ("She who is of the nature of amaurosis"), who is none else than the grandmother of the captives, puts chains on their legs. She then firmly locks the prison door and impresses on the prison guards the need to be extremely watchful all the more so as these people have killed her children, as had the youth's father before. The five prison guards who are the five "poisons" as the instinctual has traditionally been assessed and which are, figuratively speaking, the "chains" put on the prisoners, respond that they certainly will do so. The youth's entreaty to let him go free is met with scorn:[93] "As long as we have this our body we have strong desires and do not feel the need to have done with our food and wealth and friends and sons and daughters, our country and our occupations. Moreover, even those who have embraced a religious life do not understand (what you mean by saying that) there is no self.[94] Tied up in the shackles of their egological self,[95] they do not stand free of them. We even know better than you because sentient beings have been duped before by the trash (you try to sell us)." There is a subtle link between the old woman's accusing the captives of the murder of her children and the demon's calling them murderers incarnate. What the captives had done and were likely to do again was to disregard the "flesh,"[96] the tangibly sensuous and sensual, in favor of an impalpable vision of beauty and wholeness. The dramatic encounter with the dark, instinctual and demoniacal forces and the resultant imprisonment of the bright, spiritual forces in the youthful hero intimates that he had run afoul of the concrete reality of being. He had to come to grips with it by learning the hard way (for which reason he was sent away from "home" by his parents). Nonetheless, the instinctual and demoniacal forces concentrated in the figure of the old woman, the youth's "grandmother," still have some (spiritual) ties with their grandchild. These, too, have to come to grips with reality by yielding up the light ("the flame that will not quite die," though almost on the point of extinction) they had prevented from shining brightly.

The demon's retinue that serves his "interests," inspired, as it were, by the old woman,[97] is the host of the emotions that, unlike the four great catalysts,[98] literally and figuratively pollute and poison the atmosphere and everything in it.[99] There are eighty-(four) thousand[100] such pollutants of which twenty-(one) thousand, personified as male demons, are the offspring of resentment,[101] another twenty-(one) thousand, personified as female demons, are the offspring of passion,[102] still another twenty-(one) thousand, personified as snake-demons that may be either male or female, are the offspring of spiritual darkness,[103] and lastly, there are twenty-(one) thousand demons in whom the above mentioned three poisons are equally present.[104] The five attendants from among this crowd, who take hold of the youth and his companions, are the traditional quincunx of passion, hatred, dullness, arrogance, and jealousy. Among them dullness is the center from which the remaining four branch out.

This prison world of the emotion-pollutants, constituting the level of organismic mentation[105] in its somatosensory (metabolic and neural) complexity from which the higher levels of psychic (mental-spiritual) life evolve, is symbolized by an old woman. She as the generatrix of all psychic life is therefore also the "grandmother" of the youth thereby also symbolizing the thrust toward spirituality and the emancipation from the dominance of the instinctual. Representing the older (instinctual) layer of the psyche and its considerable energy she obstinately attempts to curtail any deviation from the old established patterns and, if she gets the chance as in this meeting with her grandchild, she is going to reinstate and reinforce them. In vain the youth tries to argue with her. When he threatens her to call in an army she tauntingly tells him to go ahead and that she will not bow to his threats.

Three visitors now appear on the scene.[106] They are what in abstract terms we would call the "principle of communication" or an "ultracycle" as "a model for the learning process in general."[107] According to a gloss, these three visitors are the Vinaya, Sutra, and Abhidharma sections of the Buddhist canon that were primarily meant to act as catalysts, activating the potential in learning more about ourselves in order to facilitate our pursuing of the way leading to wholeness.[108] The youth tells these visitors what his parents had told him about where to go and from whom to get help, and he hands them a letter which they promise to deliver. It is here that the youth speaks of himself as what he really is, not a mere bundle of emotion-pollutants that remain largely self-expressive and self-presentational ("behavioral"), but a spiritual being in its nascent state, a kind of entelechy,[109] or pre-existent supraconscious intensity informing the future course of its own development that at this stage needs every available help so as to have beneficial consequences for others.[110] By personally asking the "outcasts" for help, the youth not only acknowledges them as his kinsmen but also raises what had been his inferior function(s) to the level of friendly and helpful auxiliary function(s).[111]

The rescue action takes up "three days," but what is meant by this phrase has nothing to do with clock time. Interchangeably used with "three instants," this phrase points to a reawakening of the experiencer to himself and is descriptive of a sense of the psychic potential's self-intensification associated with visionary experiences of a brilliant light as intimated by the rising of the sun. This self-intensification occurs in the reverse order of its self-diminishing, its becoming "embodied" or enfolded in sheaths of its own making:[112] the whole's pure and primal symbolicalness becomes its spontaneous presence that displays itself to itself in complex self-similar patterns[113] (fractals) of incredible beauty. This reverse movement of the whole's becoming ever more self-reflexive is said to be such that[114]

> In one instant (the whole's) lighting-up in complex self-similar patterns ceases;
> In one instant (the whole's) lighting-up as a spontaneous presence comes about;
> In one instant the reality of (the whole's) pure and primal symbolicalness is seen.

The actual rescue action begins at dawn with the arrival of the "outcasts" and their armies. "Dawn" symbolizes the rising of the experiencer's "inner light" and the "arrival of the armies" points to the aided arousal of the psychic energy from now on becoming ever more intense in its cognitive capacity. This experience is felt and imaged as the smashing of the prison door whereby the intensification of the cognitive capacity as the indispensable prerequisite for a deeply felt understanding[115] of wholeness is given its first opportunity to take effect. A gloss explains this smashing of the prison door as a relinquishing of the body with the enigmatic word

"body" explicated in a subsequent note by Klong-chen rab-
'byams-pa to the next step in the rescue operation of the
"chains being broken." According to him these are the chains
of the materiality-bound egologically circumscribed subject-
object structure.[116] The materiality involved is but the low-
intensity psychic energy that manifests itself in the ingrained
tendencies to embark on discursive ventures.[117] The smashing
of the prison-door, the relinquishing of the body, and the
breaking of the chains of the materiality-bound subject-
object structure intimate, in the absence of a body-mind dualism in Buddhist rDzogs-chen teaching, a gradual process of
"psychification" and "irrealization of the body," as suggested
by C. G. Jung,[118] rather than an ordinary out-of-the-body
experience. The banishment of the old woman intimates that
in the dimension of the *lumen naturale*, which is the unre-
stricted working of the whole's high-level originary awareness, a low-level cognitive activity is literally out of place.

Concomitantly with these three rescue operations that, if
we may say so, occur at the deepest level of the psyche, three
other rescue operations take place on a slightly more overt
level of the psyche. There is first the unhorsing of five riders,
a theme we have met before.[119] This is followed by the
imprisonment of the grandmother's children and the execu-
tion of the demon's attendants. But who are the grandmother's children about whom the story had been singularly
silent?

There exists a certain ambiguity concerning the phrase
"the grandmother's children" because the Tibetan word *bu*
can also be understood in the singular as *a* child or
son/grandson, but possibly it is used here as a word that
merely refers to a close (blood) relationship. A gloss in the
text itself and the explanations by Klong-chen rab-'byams-pa
and rGod-kyi ldem-'phru-can favor the idea of taking this
word in the singular. According to the gloss in the text the
imprisonment means that "the low-level intensity of the cognitive capacity dissolves in the (whole's) supraconscious ecstatic intensity."[120] Klong-chen rab-'byams-pa explains the

imprisonment as "the supraconscious ec-static intensity, having recognized itself as what it is, is put into the prison of self-cognition beyond which it cannot go";[121] and rGod-kyi ldem-'phru-can understands the imprisonment as "in the jungle of (his) low-level cognitive capacity that is like some oppressive darkness, (the experiencer) has regained (his) supraconscious ec-static intensity that like the sun having risen."[122] While these explanations may be said to provide a valid phenomenological description of a deeply felt experience, there is still another possible interpretation with distinct political overtones already found in rDzogs-chen literature. This interpretation is contained in a terse statement serving as an advice to maintain psychic-spiritual stability:

> The king has to be seated on his throne;
> The minister has to be put into prison;
> Thereby the populace is automatically pacified.[123]

In rDzogs-chen literature, the "king" has always been considered to be a symbol of the supraconscious ecstatic intensity that in its *Ek-stasis* acts as the ordering principle in the evolution of the universe through what is the individuation process in the human individual. In this process, the "teacher" plays an indispensable role by acting as a guiding image in the true sense of the word by being the inner light of humanness, the individual's *Innerlichkeit* that makes visible, like in a mirror, the radiance of its intensity. By contrast, the minister is the individual's mentation that is more of the nature of a trouble-maker stirring up the senses, the populace, into perceiving what presences in a sort of misplaced and affect-toned concreteness. Thus, Padmasambhava elaborates:[124]

> The king's becoming seated on his throne is tantamount to his becoming confirmed in his autonomy (*vis-à-vis* his environment) The minister is mentation; provided that the creative dynamics in the supraconscious ecstatic intensity does not lose itself in the storminess (of the instinctual, it does not become conceptually divided

(against itself) and in its being without conceptual divisions it (stands in its own) radiance.[125] This is like when the minister has been put into prison and there is no cogitating intellect and ego-logical subject as agent. [Stating it differently], as long as (mentation) has not separated from the body there is breathing; since this is the horse (on which the supraconscious ecstatic intensity rides, it is like the minister. To have him put into prison means that while the storminess of conceptual divisons is still there it is unable to rage. The five senses are like the populace that does all the work. At this time [when it is not made to slave] it stays in its radiance and conceptually undivided. That is (what is meant by saying that) the populace has come to rest.

We might note that Klong-chen rab-'byams-pa, who likes to compare psychic life with political organization,[126] states explicitly—"mentation is low-level cognitive intensity";[127] the reason is that mentation is ego-logically narrowed down and rigidified. However, in order not to fall into the trap of misplaced concreteness we must remind ourselves of the fact that this "psycho-political" process takes place on the highest level of an individual's psychic activity, the level of the supraconscious ecstatic intensity that in its self-reflexivity creates the symbols through which it re-creates its world.[128]

Set free from the prison of enworldedness by the help of what had been the nuances of his inferior function, the youth hurries home. His return journey is his experiencing the luminous forces of wholeness that work in and through him in his psychized being, with eyes that "see" and in this seeing occasion the way home[129]—an inward journey, described in the concrete terms of the external world, but experienced through the imaged feelings and felt images as an intrapsychic process. On his return, the youth meets his sister carrying the flowers she had gathered from the palace of the ruler of the thirty-three gods at the peak of the experienceable world-system from where the "way," if this is still a correct term, opens into the beyond-Being. The re-union of brother and sister marks the transcendence of both the mundane from which the brother had retrieved the light that he had been, and the divine from which the sister had gathered the flowers that are her coming into full bloom. This intrapsychic process is explicated by Klong-chen rab-'byams-pa in cryptic and elliptic terms that emphasize the intensification of the luminous character of the experience and only incidentally refer to the illumining source or "lamp" to the effect that[130]

> By having seen (through a visionary gaze) Being's possibilizing dynamics, the lighting-up of (what is the youth's) own country (or: cognitive domain) as the brilliance of the *lumen naturale*, the flowers brought by the youth's sister (turn out to be) the lamp (whose light) as a measure of the intensity of the experience also marks its limit.

By contrast, rGod-kyi ldem-'phru-can[131] explicates this difficult passage as the re-union of a child with its mother, the youth or the supraconscious ecstatic intensity being the child and the cognitive capacity in its intensification as an appreciative-inspiring acumen being the mother, in terms of two lamps whose specifications differ from the standard presentation, which goes to show that a literal-mechanistic approach to these intrapsychic processes is self-defeating, if not nonsensical. rGod-kyi ldem-'phru-can's words are:

> (This passage presents in) symbolic diction the re-union of the supraconscious ecstatic intensity, a self-originated lamp, similar to a (mother's) child (son), with the appreciative-inspiring cognitive capacity (as the child's mother), the lamp that is (the whole's) field-like expanse, shining in the glow of five originary awareness modes.[132]

Adagio: Interlude

The parents' joy of seeing their offspring again is heightened by the awareness that they have outgrown their childhood and have become fully "functional" in the sense that they visibly bring forth the light that had invisibly been theirs. This activity of theirs is metaphorically spoken of in terms of "lamps" with the emphasis on the function of their spreading light rather than on the material object so called. Hence, in this context, the lamps are not even mentioned by their respective names but by their illumining activity that reflects the principle of complementarity in which the opposites include each other, neither dominating the one or the other nor either being subordinate to the one or the other, and which points to a universal connectedness and mutual correspondence in their degrees of intensity. Nonetheless, for brevity's and intelligibility's sake we cannot do without referring to these lamps as a sort of shorthand expression for complex phenomena. Two lamps have been singled out because of their importance for the visionary experience that is at the heart of this story. The one, the *thig-le stong-pa'i sgron-ma*, occurs under this name in all texts that discuss the various (usually four) lamps,[133] the other, the *dbyings rnam-par dag-pa'i sgron-ma*, is not at all mentioned by this name (that seems specific to the sNying-thig tradition as developed at some later stage), but is referred to by the term *rig-pa dbyings-kyi sgron-ma* under which name two distinct, though interrelated, lamps are understood. The one is *rig-pa* whose specifications as *thig-le* and/or *stong-pa* and/or (*rdo-rje*) *lu-gu-rgyud* are so many experienceable nuances of one and the same "thing"— the "lamp" that is the lighting-up and alightness, the whole's supraconscious ecstatic intensity. The other is *dbyings*, the lighting-up and alightness of the whole having assumed a field-like expanse.[134] Both *dbyings* and *rig-pa* in their inseparability[135] have each a dual aspect:[136]

> *dbyings* has two aspects: an inner field-like expanse and an outer field-like expanse.
> The outer field-like expanse is the (cloudless) sky; the inner field-like expanse is a bright (bifurcated) lamp.[137]
> *rig-pa*, too, is twofold: one aspect of it (the *thig-le*) is

its outward glow (*gdangs*); (the other aspect) is the "stuff" (*ngo-bo*) which it is made of (that is, the *rdo-rje lu-gu-rgyud*).[138]

The "stuff" to which reference is made is, as noted previously, Being's nothingness that also is its fulness, similar to the ever seething quantum vacuum of modern physics.[139] The seething is the excitation of this field in an effulgence that confirms us as being *luminous* beings and, since this lighting-up of Being uses our eyes as its organ or medium,[140] it is through them that it makes whatever becomes the "phenomenal" to be visible in its sensuous field.[141] It is the field's excitation, its energy fluctuation, its supraconscious ecstatic intensity that is intimated by the term *rdo-rje lu-gu-rgyud*. Here *rdo-rje*,[142] the "diamond," symbolizes the indestructible and basic reality that underlies and, as its preciousness, pervades all that has emerged from it and constitutes what we call "world"; and *lu-gu-rgyud* symbolizes the "continuity (*rgyud*) of the seething or bubbling-up (*gu*) of the ripples in a lake (*lu*) that neither increases nor decreases."[143] However, this seemingly restful picture of a calm lake with ripples passing over its surface must not allow us to overlook its tremendous dynamics. The bubbling-up is more in the manner of an incentive to envision and cultivate the vision of the emergence of Being's design, its anthropic gestaltism, out of its (field-like) expanse—like ripples in a lake[144] following a course set by the dynamics in it. This dynamics is none other than the ecstatic intensity symbolized by the son/brother who is given the title rDo-rje lu-gu-rgyud 'dren-pa. The term *'dren-pa* indicates that he is the "leader" in creating the future.

The luminous quality of this supraconscious ecstatic intensity, experienced as a bubbling-up in various shapes and patterns such as pearls which are strung together or garlands of flowers that move in the wind,[145] is matched by the luminous quality of the "field" of which it is its excitation. This luminous expanse fans out like a peacock's tail whose colorful luster intertwines with the luster in the ecstatic gaze, or spreads like the ripples in a pond into which a pebble has been thrown.[146] This expanse is envisioned as an infinite sphere that by its very dynamics becomes a vortex sphere[147] whose farthest reaches are imaged as forming a halo shimmering in the colors of the rainbow, or, more concretely, as forming a fence safeguarding the individuation process as a holistic phenomenon in which its "intensity" and its "expanse" are correlated to each other. This expanse, symbolically referred to as a lamp is described as[148]

> having a luster of its own that has no (definable) periphery; having a radiance that has no object-(like status); having a fence that is not a constructed one;[149] having a halo that is not a painted one; having a cognitive domain that is as yet not defined; and having an as-yet-unmapped dimension of light.

Surrounding the whole with a halo of supernatural light shimmering in five colors it is the daughter/sister who maintains the coherence of what later turns out to be ourselves as individuated beings. Like her brother she, too, is a shining lamp. But while her brother presents the intensity of light, she is the immense diffusion of light, and hence is given the title Mu-khyud 'dzin. Intensity and diffusion intertwine. In abstract terms we may speak of a quantum vacuum bubbling with energy or of a photon field and its excitation without which we would live in a pretty dark world; the anthropomorphic diction of brother and sister introduces a human element and lets us participate in and sense as well as understand the intimacy of the complementarity of masculinity and femininity that, in the final analysis, each of us is.[150] Stating the problem differently, we may say that what He stirs up She holds together, and in so doing both are active creating themselves as luminous forces ("lamps") and thereby evoking a meaningful world in which the old dualism of active and passive has become utterly redundant.

Presto: Finale

The story now returns to the teacher Me-long-can who had drawn the attention of those who lived in his luminous realm to the imaginary and yet realistic Mt. Malaya from which the two children of luminous parents had been sent away into the insufferably dark world of demoniac forces and the balmy semidark or semilucid[151] world of divine figures, and to which they returned as bearers of light—"lamps" whose bright luster intermingles in a revitalized unity. The reappearance of the teacher at this point of the story is of crucial importance. It emphasizes the fact that the individuation process has not yet run its course and that a further "ascent" marking an evolutionary unfolding of life, is necessary and about to take place. As a first step in this direction, the son/brother and daughter/sister had been given titles reflecting their intrinsic nature as dynamic luminosities implicitly pointing to a future to be realized; and as an indication of what still lies before them they are allusively addressed by the teacher as "noble children," their nobility lying in their being participatory agents in what constitutes the resonance domains of Being's wholeness with itself and everything else as its probabilistic projections or emanations. Although the story itself does not state which resonance domain is implied, all the evidence—the emphasis on light referring back to the whole's supraconscious ectstatic intensity, the release from the prison and murkiness of the instinctual indicating spiritual blindless and an almost total lack of ecstatic intensity, the flowering of an originary awareness mode in its specific sense of being the whole's field-like expanse of existential meanings—points to the central resonance domain that circumscribes the individual's evolutionary thrust toward individuation and/or wholeness.[152] This thrust *in*-forms, in the strict sense of the word, the individual's body-as-lived that, when energized by the power of this thrust, is his/her spirit/spirituality. It is not without significance that the ordering principle in this resonance domain as humankind's overall evolutionary thrust is spoken of in terms of the intimacy between its regent named "Illuminer" and his consort named "Mistress of the Dimension of Meanings."[153]

The teacher tells the brother-sister pair about a realm that in its lighting-up is the coming-to-presence of their own as yet unrealized potential. In this "no-man's-land" that is far from hostile and experientially constitutes a decisive phase transition,[154] the principle of creative self-organization plays an important role. The emerging self-image expresses itself in symbolic form as a crystal stūpa. Traditionally the crystal has been a symbol for purity and clarity; but it is its transparency that transcending the duality of a within and a without makes it a suitable device for understanding the dynamics of mind/consciousness/spirit. In the present context concerned with the experiencer's inner, psychic-spiritual processes the symbol of the crystal is understood as a dynamic system in its own right. In its lighting-up it introduces a directedness, a vector that indicates in which direction the new structure can be expected to move. This new structure is experienced as the emergence of that which constitutes the primordial existential structure of our being, whose multiple interconnected gestalts[155] are the preontological possibility of understanding ourselves, evoking in this understanding a world that is truly ours. It should be noted that this preontological structure is more of the nature of an undulation that remains strictly within the realm of its potential and its coherence. Only when this undulation reaches a critical phase in its intensity so as to cross its instability threshold—as when a crystal is exposed to the rays of the sun falling on it and now bursts forth in a spectrum colored light— the original intensity becomes lowered and the fragmentation of wholeness takes place in a manner in which the fragments or parts are simultaneously present with the whole.[156] While the symbol of the crystal may be said to emphasize the self-organizing *process* of the whole, the symbol of the stūpa, the most sacred architectural form in Buddhist art,[157] may be said to emphasize the *structure* into which the whole in its spirituality molds itself.[158]

Accordingly, the complex process structure of what constitutes—if this is the proper term—the core of psychic-spiritual life is mediately and perceptibly presented by the complex architecture of the stūpa whose five tiers—there may be more dependent on how many levels in the hierarchical organization of the psyche one assumes and relates to architectural patterns—are here understood as the five luminosities in and through which the originary awareness modes are experienced. Each luminosity is not a monadic entity, rather it is itself a fivefold of intertwining luminosities that share in the original fivefold's vertical and horizontal presence. Vertically these luminosities are the five tiers of the stūpa and horizontally they are the stūpa's ground plan as a centered four or *maṇḍala*. In this way, the two notions of a circle and a quaternity are uniquely combined. In speaking of these luminosities as "persons,"[159] they are recognized as psychic forces with whom the experiencer can establish meaningful relationships. The four mirrors, which the luminous persons place at the four points of the compass, reflect back on the original mirror in which the whole mirrors itself in its becoming "conscious" of itself. It hardly needs pointing out that the circumference of the stūpa is a halo of light with which the whole, "seen" in its expanse, rather than "felt" in its intensity, surrounds itself.

The brother-sister pair standing on the summit of Mt. Malaya, the highest level of their worldy rational, emotional, and spiritual knowledge, has to enter into this vast expanse that unfolds before their eyes. Once inside they climb a jeweled staircase, symbolic of an intensification of the experiential process that is both a deepening and a heightening of an existential awareness.

Reaching the top landing of the staircase that is the pinnacle of the stūpa, the brother-sister pair comes face to face with the teacher 'Od mi-'gyur-ba, "Light-Invariant," from whose right foot a rope of light extends that "touches" and "draws" the brother-sister pair close to the figure of the teacher, before whom, as has been and still is customary in a teacher-disciple relationship, they bow their heads and touch his feet in reverence and awe. The fact that only the teacher's right foot is mentioned suggests that he sits in the royal *ārdhaparyanka* pose, in which one leg is drawn up and the other stretched out.

His name indicates that the light he is remains invariant and is a light that is pre-existent and supraordinate to the "phenomenon" light, and its invariance indicates that it does not change into anything else but itself under any and all transformations it may undergo. Lest the term "invariance" evokes the idea of it being something static, it should be borne in mind that this light is the triune dynamics of wholeness as may be gleaned from the statement that

> the intensity-"stuff" (of wholeness) unfolds into a gestalt, the ownmostness (of wholeness) unfolds into light, and the spirituality (of wholeness in its resonating) unfolds into rays (of light).[160]

The presence of this invariant light evokes, on the part of its experiencer, different feelings toward it and hence is spoken of in different terms, each in its own way and in images that are anthropomorphic in character, conveying a salient feature of this feeling. Frequently this invariant light is spoken of as "protector,"[161] intimating one's feeling secure in His/its presence; less frequently as "conqueror,"[162] intimating one's victory over the darker and negative forces at work in us. But most prominent among the various appellations are the "teacher"[163] from whose example we learn how to become humanly and fully alive, and the "'Buddha' process structure"[164] that, in the final analysis, is our growing up. As the principle of evolution pervasive of the universe and ourselves as an integral aspect of it, whether we speak of it in terms of a "light-invariant" or in terms of a "process structure,"[165] it is more intimately felt in and recognized by us through the archetypal image of an "ancestor"[166] or, as in this story, a "Father" who is not some fearful concretely human "father" figure—"be not afraid of it(s light)" is the advice the teacher Me-long-can gives the brother-sister pair—but a needed guiding image in the individuation process. The equivalence of light-invariant and ancestor is clearly expressed in the following passage:[167]

> Since [the whole] surpasses the countless process structures in their visible concreteness, but rises and emerges in the deeply felt understanding of what they all mean, (it is) the ancestor of all "Buddha" process structures.
>
> Since [the whole] ceaselessly radiates in the auto-effulgence of its originary awareness mode(s) and since (its) supraconscious ecstatic intensity that antedates all (effulgences) and in its auto-manifestation does not change but remains what it is, (it is) the primordial "Buddha" process structure Light-invariant.

But this evolutionary principle imaged as "Father" Light-Invariant, does not operate in a vacuum, but in a *plenum* that words cannot fathom or adequately describe,[168] and that somehow is something larger and, maybe, earlier—"a house made of crystal and having eight doors,"[169] as the story states. This house is the "spontaneous presence"[170] of Being with its immense wealth of possibilities[171] that is and in which the bountiful "Mother" of the brother-sister pair lives. It is precisely because of these possibilities she presents that she is so aptly called "She who lights up in the multiplicity (of what is to become the phenomenal world)." This multiplicity of luminous presencings that tend to externalize themselves and become separated from their source through the experiencer's not recognizing them for what they are, namely, self-presentations of the whole's spontaneous and luminous presence, are like children running away from their mother and going astray into the mistaken concretizations and identifications that make up their and, by implication, our enworldedness, from which eventually they have to break away through understanding what these are and to return to their mother.[172]

But with the return of the brother-sister pair to their "mother" their journey has not yet come to an end. They have to proceed to a precious house that is their legitimate home—Being, in its nothingness, its pure and primal symbolicalness that in its preciousness (precisely because of it not being some opaque thing) is what words, even those of poets, are unable to fathom or to convey.

Taking up the advice of their teacher whose name Melong-can once again intimates his capacity to reveal wholeness for its visionary understanding, the brother-sister pair sets out on their journey home. This journey of the brother-sister pair, who themselves are of the nature of a supramundane light, is described in symbols of light spanning the cosmos. The rays of the sun are the rays of their spirituality that becomes their steed that will speed them on; the rainbow, the five-colored lighting-up of their luminous pristinely cognitive being, becomes the saddle; and a string of pearls, the tendency of the whole to break up into the fragmentary pieces of rational dichotomies, becomes the girth that prevents the saddle from slipping and the riders from falling to the ground from which they will have to get up again not without pain. Holding in their hands a crystal as a dagger, symbolic of their exercising the clarity of their appreciative-discriminative acumen, they ride over the sky whose orb, the immensity and openness of wholeness, is the way that leads them to their precious home without presenting any obstacles. If anything can be said of its symbolicalness, its openness-nothingness that is fulness, it is the intimate immediacy of the lived-through experience of supraconscious ecstatic intensity.

Notes

1. This story forms the fortieth chapter in the *Rig-pa rang-shar*, pp. 567–578. There its title *yongs-su bstod-pa* (Enthusiastic Praise) has little to do with the content of the story, but merely refers to the response of the audience. The story is taken up with additional notes by Klong-chen rab-'byams-pa, *Theg-mchog Dgongs-pa zang-thal*, vol. 1, pp. 325–330. A more "polished" version is given by rGod-kyi ldem-'phru-can, *Theg-mchog Dgongs-pa zang-thal*, vol. 2, pp. 609–630. Here the teacher-narra-

tor is said to be *rdo-rje sems-dpa'*. This name is explicated in the *Rig-pa rang-shar*, p. 448 as "the supraconscious ecstatic intensity that understands both its own reality and that of others."

2. On this term, see chapter 1, p. 36 n. 8.

3. The Sanskrit equivalent for this word is *mahācakravāḷa*. It is less frequently used than the word *cakravāḷa*. In Indian mythology, it refers to the nine mythical mountain ranges encircling the earth with Mount Meru as the central mountain. The present text does not make any reference to a mountain or a mountain range, but speaks of a "country" (*yul*) whose vastness suggests the idea of an infinite sphere whose circumference (*khor-mo-yug*) is nowhere.

4. This sentence intimates a progressive interiorization. It moves from the immensity of the "infinite sphere," the external "physical" world, into the immensity of a "huge swamp," the internal "psychic" world with its emotions and rationalistic notions, and from there into the "spiritual" world of the *lumen naturale*. The Tibetan term *"mar-me,"* which the dictionaries state to mean "butter lamp," has here been rendered by "flame" because the emphasis is on the light that comes from it, not on the vessel as which the word "lamp" is defined in the West.

5. "Being endowed with an inner luster." The term *mdangs* indicates an inner glow that is on the verge of becoming an effulgence (*gdangs*). According to *mKha'-yang*, vol. 2, pp, 227f., it is threefold in conformity with the triune dynamics of Being. Each luster develops into a probability structure or gestalt and together they form a co-ordinated hierarchy.

6. "Being of the nature of a mirror." This phrase, serving the double purpose of being the personal name of the teacher (*ston-pa*) and describing his function as a revealer, is intended to emphasize his character of being primarily a guiding image, not a concrete person. He soon disappears, but later in the story, at a critical moment, he reappears. In the *Thig-le gsang-ba'i brda'i rgyud* (sDe-dge ed., vol. 25, fols. 49b–53b), fol. 50b, the qualification "being of the nature of a mirror," here used in connection with the guiding image of the teacher, is one among three such qualifications used in connection with archetypal Man (*khye'u*) who moves over the realms set up and is revealed in a panoramic vision by these dynamic qualifications. They are in an ascending order "being of the nature of a mirror" (*me-long-can*), revealing what we call the "physical world," "being of the nature of a rainbow" (*'ja'-mtshon-can*), displaying aesthetic possibilities before the experiencer's gaze, and "being of the nature of a jewel" (*nor-bu-can*), intimating the experiencer's value experience. The extremely concise and cryptic account in this work goes on to

say that "in the realms of archetypal Man the seed of the Demon Halika nag-po will ripen into the corruption of the flesh (*sme-sha*). Four potters (*rdza-mkhan-gyi bu*) will water and spread manure over these realms whose crop has no truth in it." The similarity of this account with the one of the Sethian Gnostics is unmistakable. See Benjamin Walker, *Gnosticism*, p. 49. We shall meet the Demon Halika nag-po as the leader of evil forces later on in our story. In the present account, he, like the Demiurg, the leader of the archons, in Gnosticism, has subordinate archons—the four potters who may well be the sons (*bu*) of the demiurg (*rdza-mkhan*). I would suggest that the four potters are the four *Māras* (Tib. *bdud*) or deadening forces—the deadening force that is the complexity of our organismic organization (*phung-po'i bdud*, Skt. *skandhamāra*), the deadening force of our instinctual-affective drives (*nyon-mongs-pa'i bdud*, Skt. *kleśamāra*), the deadening force of our intellectualistic and overevaluated notions (*lha'i bu'i bdud*, Skt. *devaputramāra*), and the deadening force of our mortality ('*chi-bdag-gi bdud*, Skt. *mṛtyumāra*).

7. In Indian literature, Mt. Malaya is famous for its medicinal trees, sandalwood trees, and snakes. Here, according to a gloss, it refers to the visionary's body that is as much "physical" as it is "spiritual." The top of the mountain indicates the person's head. The duality of "body" and "head" involves a further duality of the "heart" as the seat of the supra-conscious ecstatic intensity of Being-in-its-beingness and the "brain" as the seat of the diverse (cognitive) functions of this intensity, the originary awareness modes. These in particular are likened to a lake that as water is calm but as waves is agitated. Together, the heart and the brain, the supra-conscious ecstatic intensity and the originary awareness modes work through a person's eyes that are located in the head, although it is the whole body (over which the senses are spread) that "sees'.

8. *rgya-mtsho mu-khyud-can* might also be rendered as "a lake with a halo." To emphasize the luminous character of this "lake of originary awareness modes" as well as its "closure," for this closure or periphery that also applies to each awareness mode's delimitation (*mu-khyud*), the term '*od-kyi mu-khyud* " a closure that is of pure light" is used. See *Seng-ge rtsal-rdzogs*, pp. 266, 317; *Nyi-zla kha-sbyor*, p. 222. This halo that also may be a double halo (*mu-khyud ra-ba*) is said to be round (*zlum-po*). See *Seng-ge rtsal-rdzogs*, p. 355.

9. The narrator is very careful in the choice of his words. Here he uses the terms *yab* and *yum* "Father" and "Mother," which an outdated reductionist Western linguistics said to be merely "honorific" terms. In the Tibetan context, these terms indicate the humanly intelligible crystallization of the masculine and feminine principles operating throughout the

universe and thus point to the presence of a "spiritual" (and hence primary) dimension in a person's physical enframement. These terms are used when the children address their parents in and through whom they sense the presence of something larger. Otherwise the narrator uses the common, colloquial terms *pha* and *ma*.

10. Generally speaking this name corresponds to the Sanskrit name Kāśyapa which, when translating it into their language, the Tibetans analyzed into Sanskrit *kāś* "to shine brilliantly" and *pa* "to protect." Hence, this name is here to be understood "literally" as "Guardian of the Light."

11. Skt. Vajravarāhī. The term *rdo-rje* (Skt.*vajra*) "diamond" indicates indestructibility, and the term *phag-mo* (Skt.*varāhī*) "sow" is split into *phag* "swine" and *mo* "woman," and is explicated to the effect that, just as a swine does not distinguish between pure and impure, "She" does not bother about good and evil but stands above this dichotomy, and as woman "She" is the mother of all and everything. See Ngag-dbang bstan-'dzin rdo-rje, *mKha'-'gro bde-chen rgyal-mo'i sgrub–gzhung-gi 'grel-pa*, p. 18. Her iconography is given in *mKha'-yang*, vol. 2, pp. 255f.

12. *bdud nag-po*. The Tibetan term *bdud* is the translation of Sanskrit *Māra*, who is a symbol for all that is deadening. His characterization as "black" (*nag-po*, Skt. *kāla*) intimates the viciousness of this demon who seems to combine both Indian and Gnostic ideas. For further details, see also p. 116 n. 6.

13. They live on the top of the world-mountain Meru, their ruler is Sakra. His palace bears the name Vaijayanta. See *Abhidharmakośa* III 65. The *sPros-bral don-gsal*, fol. 2a is slightly different and more elaborate.

14. "Black Halika." In Indian mythology, Halika is the name of a serpent demon. There can be no doubt that the name is related to the term *ha-la nag-po* that means "aconite."

15. The text has *a-phyi* "grandmother" that a gloss here explains as the root of the instinctual-affective. I have changed this term to *rgan-mo* "old woman," for this is usually used with her name. See above chapter 1, p. 34 n. 12.

16. "Pile of Valuables." The name is spelled differently in different passages of this story: *rin-chen spungs-pa*, *rin-po-che'i spungs-pa*. A gloss praphrases it by *tsitta*, an experiential term that defies any translation. Symbolically we may speak of it as "the Citadel of the Heart" (*tsitta rin-po-che'i gzhal-yas* in *mKha'-snying*, vol. 1, p. 29; *tsitta rin-po-che'i sbubs* in *mKha'-yang*, vol. 2, p. 378). The name of this "country" that also is the name of one of the seventeen rDzogs-chen Tantras has found its hermeneutical interpretation in *Bi-ma snying-thig*, vol. 2, pp. 99ff.

17. *khye'u rig-byed.* The term *khye'u* means a "litle man" and occurs more frequently in the compound *khye'u chung*, frequently used by Padmasambhava in the sense of archetypal Man. See also introduction, pp. 19f. In the present context, the term *rig-byed*, here rendered as "perceptive," intimates the "rousing of the spark that will eventually turn into the flame of a supraconscious ecstatic intensity." Instead of *rig-byed* more frequently *kun-rig* is used, suggesting that this archetype is such "intensity through and through." The subsequent "fate" of this "youngster" reminds us of the "crysalide entity," as which Faust is received and admitted to the "choir of blessed boys." See Johann Wolfgang von Goethe, *Faust*, part II, verse 11,982. However, the Buddhist conception goes one step further.

18. "He who channels (the psychic energy) into a series of impulses (that transform themselves) into gestalt experiences." Instead of *rdo-rje lu-gu-rgyud*—the term *rdo-rje* intimating its indestructible (adamantine) character—*lu-gu-rgyud* alone is frequently used.

19. "She who keeps the halo from (disintegrating into mistaken identification)."

20. *rigs-kyi bu* and *rigs-kyi bu-mo.* In common parlance, these terms refer to a son and daughter of a good house (Skt. *kulaputra* and *kuladuhitṛ*). In works of an experiential character, *rigs* refers to "resonance domains" that interact with each other and are similar to Rupert Sheldrake's *morphogenetic fields* that order and shape matter so that matter will follow the patterns of these fields.

21. "Coming-to-presence in an as yet undefined pattern." According to a gloss by Klong-chen rab–'byams-pa this "presence" refers to the phase transition (*bar-do*) in which the possibilizing dynamics of wholeness (*chos-nyid*) is visually experienced.

22. "Light-Invariant." He is the archetypal image of spiritual wakefulness. See Padmasambhava's *gTer-snying rin-po-che spungs-pa'i rgyud* [abbr.: *gTer-snying*] (sDe-dge ed. vol. 2, fols. 315b–317b), fol. 316a; *sPros-bral don-gsal*, fol. 7b.

23. See above chapter 1, pp. 37 and 58f.

24. "She who lights up as the multiplicity (of the phenomenal)."

25. According to Padmasambhava, *sPros-bral don-gsal*, fol. 71b, there are four such archetypal predispositions: the traditional five organismic groupings (*phung-po*) into which an individual's complexity had been analyzed, the concrete individual's system-potential (*khams*), the tension field created in the encounter between the physical and the psychic (*skye-mched*), and the eight perceptual patterns (*tshogs-brgyad*).

According to Klong-chen rab–'byams-pa, *Yid-bzhin mdzod*, pp. 505, 692, 693, and *Bla-yang*, vol. 1, p. 310, there are three such archetypal pre-dispositions that prevent us from being truly luminous beings. He speaks of them poetically in his *Yid-bzhin mdzod*, p. 692:

> Once the three archetypal predispositions that are responsible for
> the lightless presences of one's concrete body (*lus*), of one's
> existential ("psychic") reality (*don*), and of one's contextual
> dimension (*yul*) have dissolved (into the dynamic openness-
> nothingness of wholeness)
> One's existence as a *Gestalt* (*sku*) shines brightly in the
> completeness of its qualities that is the spontaneity (of
> wholeness), like
> The flame in a container that has been smashed or a lotus flower
> that is fully open.

The crucial point is the retrieval of the immediacy of experience from its place of concealment and of keeping it alive such that our body is "seen" and felt as a gestalt (*lus* → *sku*), our "psychic" reality is seen as the working of originary awareness modes (*don* → *ye-shes*), and the environment in which we live is seen as a realm of inexhaustible beauty (*yul* → *zhing-khams mi-zad-pa'i rgyan-gyi 'khor-lo*).

26. The Tibetan term *ston-pa* is both a verb and a noun. Its primary meaning is "to show," and teaching is done by showing.

27. In rDzogs-chen thought the experiencer's "body" (*lus*) is spirit (*thugs*) to the extent that it has lost much of its intensity (*rig-pa*) and as an organ of cognitive processes is primarily concerned with the conceptual (*rnam-shes*) and the instinctual-affective (*nyon-mongs*). It also is a syn-thetically organized system on and in which the various organs of sense are spread out. With the emphasis on vision as the starting point of spiri-tual life, the eye-that-"sees" is of utmost importance.

28. *Byang-chub–kyi sems thugs-(kyi) rgyud rin-po-che spungs-pa'i rgyan* (sDe-dge ed. vol. 6), fol. 345b. This work is attributed to Śrīsiṃha and his translator Vairocana. It should be noted that in its Sanskrit title (if ever it had one) *Bodhicitta-ratnakūṭa-alaṅkāra* the Sanskrit original for the Tibetan *thugs-(kyi) rgyud* is missing.

29. *Theg-mchog*, vol. 2, p. 190.

30. In this technical term, *grol* has a verbal connotation and what is going on has done so since time before time (*ye, ye-nas*). This same verbal connotation is present in the related technical term *rang-grol*, where *rang* indicates that what is going on does so by itself. There is no word in any Western language that could express the vector feeling-tone character of *grol* that is mechanically and uncomprehendingly "translated" as "free."

31. The term *dgongs-pa* is specific to rDzogs-chen (sNying-thig) thinking. It refers to a dynamic intentionality of unpremeditated concern that evolves from experience and relies on insight. Life's meaning evolves, if we may say so by paraphrasing its Tibetan cryptogram *khams-gsum yongs-grol*, in the direction of eventually standing completely free (*yongs-grol*) from the limitations set by the levels of embodied existence (*khams-gsum*). The critique of the systems that base themselves on mere approximations to wholeness and by implication confuse wholeness with their pet notions is meant to say that they do not go beyond a representation of probability and remain geared to a static state.

32. There are three such "transmissions" (*brgyud-pa*): the first that is already virtually operative before Being's holomovement sets in is termed *rgyal-ba dgongs-pa'i brgyud-pa* "the transmission of Being's meaning and purpose on the level of wholeness as it emerges in the symbol of Kun-tu bzang-po as the proto-patterning of (Being's) spiritual awakening." The second transmission is termed *rig-'dzin brda'i brgyud* "the transmission by way of symbols and gestures to those who are of a mystical bent." The third transmission is termed *gang-zag snyan-khung-du brgyud-pa* "the oral transmission among human personages." Thus, Klong-chen rab-'byams-pa's statements in *Zab–yang*, vol. 2, pp. 154, 194, 200, go ultimately back to Padmasambhava's *sPros-bral don-gsal*, fol. 68b, even if he supports them by quoting from the *Thig-le kun-gsal* (an excerpt from Padmasambhava's larger work). The boundaries between the first two transmissions are fluid: in the sNying-thig literature rDo-rje sems-dpa' (Skt. Vajrasattva) is the "larval stage" of Mi-bskyod-pa (Skt. Akṣobhya) who is a *rgyal-ba*, while Kun-tu bzang-po is irreducible to either. In extant Sanskrit works Samantabhadra (Tib. Kun-tu bzang-po) is a Bodhisattva, not a symbol of wholeness as in rNying-ma writings. An exception is Anangavajra's *Prajñopāyaviniśayasiddhi* I 27.

33. On the term *rdo-rje sems-dpa'* see also note 1.

34. In Padmasambhava's *Nam-mkha'i mtha' dang mnyam-pa'* the relationship between Kun-tu-bzang-po and rDo-rje-sems-dpa' is that between teacher and disciple.

35. On "symbolic pregnance" see introduction, p. 25 n. 49.

36. The rDzogs-chen conception of the body-as-lived as a "congeal-ment" of what is ultimately the whole's supraconscious ecstatic intensity *via* a drop in its intensity resulting in a genus- and species-specific background pattern of conscious and protoconscious life, evinces a striking similarity with Maurice Merleau-Ponty's conception of the body-proper (the corporeal scheme, later called "the flesh") as the "*expression*" of con-

scious life. See the assessment of Merleau-Ponty's idea of the body-proper and its phenomenological implications in Richard M. Zaner, *The Problem of Embodiment*, Part III: Merleau-Ponty's Theory of the Body-Proper, pp. 17–233. Thus, while the body-as-lived (*lus*) is experienced as remaining constant in its being the ongoing process of embodying consciousness/spirit (*rig-pa/rnam-shes*), one of its functions, seeing by means of the eyes (*mig*) perceives patterns (*gzugs*) that are both stable and fluid. This explains why the mountain is, metaphorically speaking, both the supraconscious ecstatic intensity (*rig-pa*) and a pattern that is as much a perceptual pattern (*gzugs*) as it is a gestalt (*sku*).

37. In his *sPros-bral don-gsal*, fol. 74a, Padmasambhava uses the phrase *ri-rab–kyi rtse-mo rgya-mtsho nyi-ma-can* which may be rendered as "the peak of the world-mountain (*ri-rab–kyi rtse-mo*) that is of the nature of a lake (*rgya-mtsho*) and of the nature of the sun (*nyi-ma-can*). The term *nyi-ma-can* has been used as the "name" of the country that is the luminous "home" of the individuated Self in the previous story. See above p. 37. Strictly speaking, in spite of the "translation" of the above quoted phrase, its intent is untranslatable. We simply have to sense the loftiness of the mountain as it imperceptibly passes into the vastness of a lake in the brightness of the sun's splendor in order to understand its rich meaning.

38. See note 28 for reference.

39. *srid-pa'i g.yo-'gul*. In rDzogs-chen literature, the term *srid-pa* is always understood as that which gives (the whole's) lighting-up (*snang-ba*) its particular restrictive meaning, emphasizing the fact that we live in an "interpreted world" (*snang-srid*). A lengthy, hermeneutical exposition of the compound *snang-srid* is given in Padmasambhava's *bDud-rtsi bcud-thig*, fol. 235a. The "interpreted world" comprises the traditional three worlds or levels of experience: the world of desires (Skt. *kāma-dhātu*, Tib.*'dod-pa'i khams*), the world of aesthetic forms (*rūpadhātu*, *gzugs-kyi khams*), and the world of no-forms (*arūpadhātu*, *gzugs-med-kyi khams*). They all are "projections" of the egological mind (*sems*).

40. *Zab–yang*, vol. 1, p. 351.

41. "Like in a lake not ruffled by the wind," as he says in *Bla-yang*, vol. 1, p. 436.

42. This important distinction between a "manipulatable" object (*gzung-yul*) and an object "coming-to-presence in its lighting-up" (*snang-yul*) has clearly anticipated Alfred North Whitehead's distinction between "perception in the mode of causal efficacy" and "perception in the mode of presentational immediacy." On this distinction see Elizabeth M. Kraus, *The Metaphysics of Experience*, pp. 72–80.

43. The Tibetan term *rgya-mtsho* means both a lake and/or an ocean and hence the term *ye-shes rgya-mtsho* can be rendered as "an ocean of originary awareness modes" in order to convey something of the vastness of its (their) scope. The image of a lake or ocean and its waves is used by Klong-chen rab–'byams-pa, *mKha'-yang*, vol. 1, pp. 397, 398. The term *ye-shes rgya-mtsho* is frequently used in *Seng-ge rtsal-rdzogs*, pp. 250, 304, 305, 333, 393. It is not without interest that one of the five originary awareness modes, ranking first in their enumeration, is the "mirror-like originary awareness mode" (*me-long lta-bu'i ye-shes*). On the relationship between water and mirror see the sensitive study by Gaston Bachelard, *Water and Dreams*, pp. 21 and passim.

44. *sGra-thal-'gyur chen-po'i rgyud*, p. 110

45. The Tibetan name of this fence-like mountain, called "Nimindhara" in Sanskrit sources, is *mu-khyud-'dzin*. The difference in terminology, *mu-khyud-'dzin* on the one hand and *mu-khyud-can* on the other hand is highly significant. The former expression shows this mountain to be a content of representational thought, the latter expression points to its experiential character. Nonetheless, the idea of a periphery forming a fence (*ra-ba*) was not forgotten, and the combination *mu-khyud ra-ba* occurs, for instance, in *Seng-ge rtsal-rdzogs*, pp. 355, 359; *sGra-thal-'gyur chen-po'i rgyud*, p. 163; *Rig-pa rang-grol*, p. 22; *Rig-pa rang-shar*, p. 574. All texts declare this periphery to be "circular" (*zlum-po*). On the symbolic meaning of the circle see J. C. Cooper, *An Illustrated Encyclopaedia of Traditional Symbols*, s.v. circle.

46. *Seng-ge rtsal-rdzogs*, p. 266: *phyogs dang bral-ba'i 'od-kyi mu-khyud zin*.

47. This term has been coined by Gaston Bachelard, *The Poetics of Space*, p. 183.

48. The Tibetan term *nam-mkha'* (Skt. *ākāśa, gagana*) means both "space" and "sky." In rDzogs-chen thought, its "precise" meaning varies with the levels of experience, roughly corresponding to what we call the "external" or "physical," the "internal" or "psychological," and the "arcane" (for which our binary mode of thinking has no term). See *dGongs-pa zang-thal*, vol. 2, p. 403; vol. 3, p. 400.

49. For reference see note 28.

50. I would suggest that this line is an interpretative interpolation and not part of the statement itself bcause it breaks the two-line verse form in which each image is presented.

51. In its strictly technical use *rab–tu mi-gnas* (Skt. *apratiṣṭhita*) means "non-localizability."

52. Dictionaries give the Sanskrit word *garuḍa* as the equivalent of the Tibetan term *khyung-chen*, which has led to endless confusion. Actually there are two terms, *khyung* and *khyung-chen*, which have to be kept apart. The Indian *garuḍa* is the mount of the god Viṣṇu; the Tibetan *khyung-chen* is never a mount. If a mount is intended the term used is *khyung*; see for instance Padmasambhava's *sNang-srid kha-sbyor*, fol. 217b. By contrast, *khyung-chen* is a symbol of the supraconscious ecstatic intensity (*rig-pa*). This symbol is frequently used in works by (or attributed to) Śrīsiṃha who, according to Klong-chen rab–'byams-pa, *gNas-lugs*, p. 68, is the much maligned Hva-shang (the Chinese opponent to the Indian Kamalaśīla at the so-called bSam-yas debate (792–794 of the common era), a historical-political hoax). and by Klong-chen rab–'byams-pa himself who not only quotes this stanza but also wrote a small text, bearing the title *khyung-chen gshogs-rdzogs* ("The full-fledged *khyung-chen* ") and preserved in *Zab–yang*, vol. 1, pp. 265–272), obviously a tribute to Śrīsiṃha's *Khyung-chen mkha'-lding* ("The *khyung-chen* hovering in the sky"), preserved in *Bi-ma snying-thig*, vol. 2, pp. 376–387.

53. Apart from obvious misspellings by the copyist, the reading of this line is uncertain. The above rendering "what curtails vision" is a compromise between *lta-ba'i spyi-rgya* and *lta-ba'i phyi-rgya*. The first version intimates the "general frame" that turns the openness of vision into the closure of dogma; the second version speaks of an "outer frame" that limits vision.

54. Its triune hierarchical organization is summed up in the technical term *sku 'od ye-shes gsum-brtsegs*, which is discussed in *dGongs-pa zang-thal*, vol. 4, p. 249; *Tshig-don*, pp. 226f.; and summarized in the *Theg-pa kun-gyi spyi-phud / klong-chen rab–'byams-kyi rgyud*, fol. 111b.

55. On the hermeneutical explication of its Tibetan term rDo-rje Phag-mo see above p. 118 n. 11.

56. On the wide-spread symbol of the sow see J. C. Cooper, *An Illustrated Encyclopedia of Traditional Symbols*, s.v. swine.

57. Relatively speaking, Kun-tu bzang-mo and her consort Kun-tu bzang-po figure prominently in Klong-chen rab–'byams-pa's writings belonging to the "later" phase of rDzogs-chen; with Padmasambhava this male-female complementarity, reflecting an "earlier" phase, is expressed in the symbols of rDo-rje-'chang chen-po and rDo-rje Phag-mo.

58. "*Ek-stasis* means standing outside "one's self," and so canceling out the conditioned mind" are the words of Monica Sjöö and Barbara Mor, *The Great Cosmic Mother*, p. 52. On the same page they state evocatively, in the best sense of the word, that "Ecstasy is the dance of the individual

with the All." The "conditioned mind" of which these authors speak is our ego-logical consciousness.

59. The use of the term *bshos-pa* and the names of the partners in this union subtly intimate that the sexual act is conceived of as an ecstatic field of radiant energy, perpetually dividing itself into masculinity and femininity whilst perpetually holding the two together in the unity of a *prior intertwining*—intertwining being a term introduced and frequently used by Maurice Merleau-Ponty in his phenomenological writings. A unique blend of modern psychology and what once was called "mystical knowledge" has been presented by Louis William Meldman, *Mystical Sex*.

60. In rDzogs-chen symbolic language, they are spoken of as "lamps" (*sgron-ma*). The full implication of this symbol will be discussed later.

61. *Faust*, part II: verse 11962.

62. See also above p. 118 n. 12. As in the Sanskrit language that distinguishes between personifications of death in its more biological aspect (*māra*) and death in its mental-spiritual aspect (*mṛtyu*) the Tibetan language, too, distinguishes between *bdud* and *'chi-bdag*. In his *Chos-dbyings rin-po-che'i mdzod*, pp. 290f., Klong-chen rab–'byams-pa gives a detailed account of what is to be understood by *bdud*. He begins with the concise statement that every (egologically founded) belief in objectifiability so that what is so objectified can be thought of in rational terms and spoken of in common parlance is a deviant fragmentation (of the unity of spirit/mind) and is "the entrance into the realm of darkness that befogs the understanding of the whole's intensity-"stuff" (*ngo-bo*) being a dynamic nothingness (*zang-thal*). This belief in (rationally reductive) definability is a deadening force that fetters (*'ching-ba'i bdud*)." He then goes on to explain the "stuff" or substance of this deadening force to be the lack of or drop in the supraconscious ecstatic intensity (*ma-rig-pa*) that expresses itself in the misleading notion of all thought being dichotomic with four ramifications being of primary importance for a person's embodied life. These he illustrates by quoting from the *Rig-pa rang-grol*, pp. 35f.:

> If you are hooked on the concrete phenomena of samsara, this means that the deadening force of the conglomerate that constitutes your embodied being (*phung-po'i bdud*) is active;
> If you are hooked on the mud-slinging in disputations, this means that the deadening force of your emotional nature (*nyon-mongs-kyi bdud*) is active;
> If you are hooked on (the experience of) joy and sadness as your friends, this means that the deadening force of (your being on) an ego-trip (*lha'i bu'i bdud*) is active;

If you (are besides yourself) with a furious rage or go berserk, this means that the deadening force of death-himself (*'chi-bdag-gi bdud*) is active.

He concludes his presentation by another quotation from the same work:

When these four deadening forces have been conquered
The other deadening forces have no chance (to become active).

63. The theme of the boy's mission and his success is strikingly similar to that in the so-called Hymn of the Pearl. This gnostic tale is found in the apocryphal Acts of the Apostle Thomas where it is called "Song of the Apostle Judas Thomas in the land of the Indians." For details see Hans Jonas, *The Gnostic Religion*, pp. 112ff.; Benjamin Walker, *Gnosticism*, p.58; Kurt Rudolph, *Gnosis*, p. 29 et passim. As Benjamin Walker, *Gnosticism*, p. 169, points out: "Eastwards, Manicheism spread through Iran, Afghanistan, India, Chinese Turkestan, and Central Asia to China. It even took root in western Tibet and influenced the indigenous pre-Buddhist Bon and Lamaist religions of that country." In view of the fact that early rDzogs-chen thought evolved in areas where Gnostic ideas were rampant, this story from the *Rig-pa rang-shar* can be seen as further evidence of the intermeshing of Gnostic and Buddhist ideas. However, while from a storyteller's point of view the theme of a mission is a wonderful device, it somehow does not fit into the rDzogs-chen pattern of thought with its premise of the self-organization of Being. It therefore seems that the frame of the story was taken over from the Gnostic tale but its content was psychologically reworked. Another point to note that in the present story it is an undying flame, not a jewel, that has to be retrieved. However, the image of a jewel (*nor-bu*) is used in *sNang-srid kha-sbyor*, fols. 250b seq. There it has to be bought back from an "old woman" by the luminous archetypal Man (*khye'u chung*).

64. *ling-tog-can*. See also chapter 1, p. 62 n. 12.

65. In many respects, this image resembles C. G. Jung's notion of the "shadow." For a summary of Jung's notion see Daryl Sharp, *C. G. Jung Lexicon:*, pp. 123–125.

66. The texts therefore speak of a *lhan-cig-skyes-pa'i ma-rig-pa* and a *lhan-cig-skyes-pa'i ye-shes*. See, for instance, *mKha'-yang*, vol. 3, pp. 11, 172; *Bla-yang*, vol. 1, p. 296.

67. The spelling of this *ma-rig-pa* varies: either *kun-tu brtags-pa* "total fragmentation" or *kun-tu btags-pa* "total labeling." This "set" of three *ma-rig-pa* (*ma-rig-pa gsum*) is matched by a "set" of three hierarchically organized *ye-shes*, of which more will be said later.

68. These are primarily the "concretized" levels of the world of aesthetic forms with their welter of divine figures.

69. See above p. 118 n. 16.

70. The country's name *Rin-po-che'i phung-po* may imply the narrator's "subjective" awareness of the preciousness of his embodiment (*phung-po*), while the name *Rin-po-che spungs-pa* may contain an "objective" reference to a rDzogs-chen Tantra of the same name.

71. *Bi-ma snying-thig*, vol. 2, p. 99.

72. This term, as it stands, is the Tibetan transliteration of the Sanskrit word *citta* "mind/mentation," but in rDzogs-chen (sNying-thig) literature has lost its original granular character, and has become the infrastructure of an individual's psyche. It is imaged as a "precious palace" (*rin-po-che'i gzhal-yas*) or as a "precious envelope" (*rin-po-che'i sbubs*). See *mKha'-snying*, vol. 1, p. 29, and *mKha'-yang*, vol. 2, pp. 264, 378, respectively. In the *sGra-thal-'gyur-ba*, pp. 111, 126, and the *Seng-ge rtsal-rdzogs*, p. 258, the term *rin-chen gzhal-yas* is used. In *Zab–yang*, vol. 1, p. 300, Klong-chen rab–'byams-pa uses the term *tsitta rin-chen gzhal-yas*. Imaged as a "palace" the *tsitta* is octahedronal (*mKha'-snying*, vol. 1, p 62), intimating its relatedness to the eight perceptual patterns through which the "mind" operates. For details see my *From Reductionism to Creativity*, chapter 2.

73. On the many meanings of the word "heart" see Stephan Strasser, *The Phenomenology of Feeling*, particularly Robert E. Wood's *Introduction* to this work and the chart on p. 10.

74. The term *rin-chen sbubs*, short for *rin-po-che'i sbubs*, occurs in *sPros-bral don-gsal*, fols. 71b, 72a. Klong-chen rab–'byams-pa, *Theg-mchog*, vol. 1, p. 299, qualifies *rin-po-che'i sbubs* by *lhun-grub* "spontaneously present," and conceives of it as a process involving a starting point, a way, and a goal or destination. It is the latter that is specified, in addition to *lhun-grub*, as *gsang-ba*: *lhun-grub rin-po-che gsang-ba'i sbubs*. But in *Tshig-don*, p. 499, he uses *ka-dag* instead of *lhun-grub* and further qualifies it as *chos-sku*. Thus: *chos-sku ka-dag rin-po-che gsang-ba'i sbubs*. In *Chos-dbyings*, p. 331, this phrase is given as *ka-dag chos-sku rin-po-che gsang-ba'i sbubs*. For Klong-chen rab–'byams-pa *ka-dag* and *lhun-grub* are indivisible (*dbyer-med*) and it is only a matter of emphasis whether attention is directed on Being's pure and primal symbolicalness, its energy/intensity-"stuff" (*ngo-bo/ka-dag*) or on its spontaneous thereness or eigenstate (*rang-bzhin/lhun-grub*).

75. *Septem Sermones ad mortuos*, First Sermon.

76. On the basis of modern quantum physics, a similar idea has been put forward by Fred Alan Wolf, *Star Wave*, p.203. More recently, Danah Zohar, *The Quantum Self*, chapter fifteen, has noted the problem, but mars her insight by an attempt to save an outdated Judaeo-Christian dualism.

77. *thugs-rje.* Hermeneutically speaking this term means "the primacy (*rje*) of spirituality (*thugs*). It resonates with Being's eigenstate as the degree of Being's intensity passing through it.

78. Erich Jantsch, *Design for Evolution*, p. 99.

79. *sPros-bral don-gsal*, fol. 5a: *gzhi dang gzhi-snang chen-po*. By specifying the lighting-up as *chen-po* "great," he emphasizes this process as being holistic.

80. This is pointed out in two glosses to the text, the first by its unknown editor, the other by Klong-chen rab–'byams-pa. At the danger of oversimplification these metaphorical expressions may be said to complement each other in the sense that *shes-rab* emphasizes referential cognitions and *sgron-ma* emphasizes (their) inner illumining functions. The story itself does not say anything about the lamps at this stage but cryptically refers to them on the occasion of the hero's and the heroine's return.

81. On the many nuances in what this technical term means, see my *From Reductionism to Creativity*, s.v. *prajñā* and *shes-rab*.

82. In *Zab–yang*, vol. 1, p. 457, Klong-chen rab–'byams-pa states that "*shes-rab* is the cognitive potential (*shes-pa*) in which the creative dynamics of (the whole's) spirituality-resonance (*thugs-rje'i rtsal*) has (not yet assumed) the duality of its coming-to-the-fore and its (simultaneous) dissolving (in the dynamics of its pure potentiality, *shar-grol gnyis-med*); although there is an (ec-static) cognition of an "objective" cognitive domain (*yul rig*), there is no involvement with this domain (*yul phyir ma-'brangs*); hence the effulgent luster of the supraconcious ec-static intensity (*rig-gdangs*) is (conceptually) undivided." In his *mKha'-yang*, vol. 2, p. 378, he quotes the *Klong-gsal* to the effect that "the ownmost creative dynamics in the self-existent supraconscious ec-static intensity (*rang-byung rig-pa'i rang-rtsal*)" abides among other sets of quincunxes as a quincunx of *shes-rab*. The discrepancy between the five *shes-rab* in Klong-chen rab–'byams-pa's *mKha'-yang* (*Klong-gsal*) and his *Tshig-don*, p. 226 and the four *shes-rab* in our story and the *Rig-pa rang-shar*, pp. 555f., is easily solved. The *Klong-gsal* gives an overview of the various *shes-rab*, the "all-encompassing *shes-rab*" (*khyab–byed-kyi shes-rab*) being the fifth one; our story mentions only four because the boy as the participant in the ensuing drama is the fifth *shes-rab*.

83. *Tshig-don*, p. 226.

84. *mKha'-yang*, vol. 2, p. 382.

85. *Tshig-don*, p. 226.

86. *mKha'-yang*, vol. 2, p. 382.

87. The gloss in the *Rig-pa rang-shar* and the version of this story as recorded by rGod-kyi ldem-'phru can speak of a *sgrol-byed-kyi shes-rab*, "a psychic potential arousal that sets free," and a *gcod-byed-kyi shes-rab*, "a psychic potential arousal that cuts off." The two aspects apply to the "arousal that sets free" in *Tshig-don*, p. 226 where this arousal is defined as "since it cuts off the life of both samsara and nirvana by the possibiliz-ing dynamics of wholeness, it is called the "psychic potential arousal that sets free." The possibilizing dynamics of wholeness (*chos-nyid*) bears comparison with the electromagnetic field in modern science. In the words of B. K. Ridley, *Time, Space and Things*, p. 109: "Everywhere in the universe the electro-magnetic field is busy creating ghostly photons out of nothing and just as busily annihilating them. Everywhere the Dirac field is demoniacally creating and annihilating electron-positron [*sam-sara-nirvana, oops!* italics mine] pairs." According to the standard list of four psychic potential arousals in both *Tshig-don* and *mKha-'yang* this "arousal that sets free" is preceded by "a psychic potential arousal that dispatches" (*bskyod-pa'i shes-rab*), defined in *mKha'-yang* as "the com-ing-and-going of the luminescent aspect (in the *lumen naturale*)," whose felt understanding leads to the emancipation from samsara as detailed by the subsequent arousal, and defined in *Tshig-don* as "the dispatching of the (experiencer's) ec-static intensity into the sky-like immensity of wholeness by way of the wind-like movement of (the whole's) originary awareness."

88. The Tibetan language does not clearly distinguish between the sin-gular and the plural of a given noun, hence only the context in which the noun is used can decide its rendering in either the singular or the plural.

89. In the Sanskrit language, *puṣpa* means both "flower" and "men-struation." The same applies to the Tibetan word *me-tog*.

90. *Seng-ge rtsal-rdzogs*, p. 259.

91. *Mu-tig phreng-ba*, p. 505. A gloss explains the "lamp" as the com-ing-to-presence, the lighting-up of Being in its wholeness (*gzhi-snang*), and the "fruit" as a summary term for the three gestalts (*sku*) as the expressions and the expressed of the whole's triune hierarchically orga-nized originary awareness modes (*ye-shes*). For details of this triune hier-archy (*ye-shes (g)sum brtsegs*) see my *Matrix of Mystery*, pp. 19, 219, n. 10.

92. In rDzogs-chen thought *rgyan* marks the conclusion of a process that starts with the whole's creative dynamics (*rtsal*) and proceeds playfully (*rol*) to its conclusion (*rgyan*) that retains its dynamic character. The term *rgyan* is therefore both a noun and a verb according to Western linguistic categories. In abstract terms, we may speak of *rgyan* as "beauty." In his *sPros-bral don-gsal*, fols. 11b–12a, Padmasambhava states:

> The beauty of Being's possibilizing dynamics lies in its triune gestalt character;
> The beauty of the *chos-sku* (as its primary ornament) lies in its twofold gestalt character [consisting of *longs-sku* and *sprul-sku*] (as secondary ornaments).
> The five originary awareness modes displaying the functioning (of this complexity)
> Are said to be the beauty of both (the primary and secondary ornaments of Being's possibilizing dynamics).
> An analogy (for this complexity) is a gold ring studded with turquoises.
> The definition (of *rgyan*) according to its intrinsic differentiation is as follows:
> The fact that Being's possibilizing dynamics wears as its ornament the *chos-sku*
> Attests to its loveliness in view of its openness being a radiance.
> The fact that the *chos-sku* wears as its ornaments the five originary awareness modes
> Attests to its loveliness in its ceaselessly active qualities.
> The fact that the originary awareness modes wear as their ornaments (the whole's) spirituality/resonance
> Attests to its loveliness in leading the six kinds of sentient beings to their legitimate dwelling (of wholeness).
> Therefore, because of its loveliness one speaks of beauty.

At a much later time, g.Yung-ston rdo-rje dpal bzang-po, one of Bu-ston's (1290–1364) foremost disciples, distinguishes between the beauty provided by worldly things (*'jig-rten-pa'i rgyan*) and the beauty of the auto-presencing originary awareness modes (*ye-shes rang-snang-gi rgyan*). In his *gSal-byed me-long* (a commentary on the *gSang-ba snying-po*), fol. 23a, he says of the former that one gets satisfied by just having a look at it, and of the latter that one cannot gaze at it long enough. Furthermore, the beauty of worldly things does not elicit additional aspects of beauty, but the beauty of the auto-presencing originary awareness modes elicits additional aspects of beauty; and, lastly, the beauty of one worldly thing is eclipsed by another worldly thing, but the beauty of the auto-presencing originary awareness modes is not eclipsed by the one or the other awareness mode, but enhanced.

93. rGod-kyi ldem-'phrug-can, *dGongs-pa zang.thal*, p. 623.

94. *bdag-med.* This denial of a self in the sense of a substance is a key notion in Buddhism and is directed against the naive identification of the ego with the self, the ego being the self limited and reduced to the status of being the active pole in a subject-object structure, which, of course, is not the whole.

95. The Tibetan compound *nga-* (ego)-*bdag* (self) excellently brings out the mistaken identification of the one with the other.

96. The term *mi sha-bo*, which I have rendered as "human beings on whom we will take our revenge," contains a direct reference to flesh (*sha*) and furthermore implies that it presents a chance for retaliating the killing of someone. A gloss to the old woman's children states that the "body of flesh (*sha*) and skin (*lpags*)" is meant.

97. Though not explicitly stated the well-known Buddhist complementarity of the "effectiveness principle" (*thabs*) and the "inspiration-appreciation principle" (*shes-rab*) is easily recognizable in the male figure of the demon and the female figure of the old woman, both operating in their restrictedness to the instinctual in negative feedback loops.

98. They are love, compassion, joyfulness, and equanimity. Their functions have been detailed in my *Kindly bent to ease us*, vol. 1, pp. 107–122.

99. In their polluting aspect, they are referred to as *nyon-mongs* (Skt. *kleśa*), in their poisoning aspect as *dug* (Skt. *viṣa*). It is unfortunate that Western psychology does not draw a distinction between catalysts and emotions.

100. The standard phrase is "eighty thousand" (*stong-phrag brgyad-cu*), but when broken down into four units, each unit contains "twenty-one thousand" (*stong-phrag nyi-shu-rtsa-gcig*) pollutants.

101. This term, *zhe-sdang*, is difficult to render by a single word since it comprises too many nuances including irritation, embitterment, rancor, enmity, hatred and many more character defects.

102. The same observations as in the case of *zhe-sdang* (see preceding note) also hold for *'dod-chags*, which may mean desire, attachment, concupiscence, sexual passion, possessiveness, and many other related affective vagaries.

103. *gti-mug*. This word, too, has many different connotations, such as insensitivity, dullness and, above all, spiritual darkness and/or blindness. These snake-demons, *klu* in Tibetan, *nāga/nāgī* in Sanskrit, live in rivers and lakes where they guard treasures. On the whole they are friendly, but become fierce only when they are angered.

104. This numerical assessment of the pollutants as the major hindrances on a person's spiritual growth is very old. On a more modest scale, it is found in Vasubandhu's *Abhidharmakośa* V 4–5. For details see my *From Reductionism to Creativity*, pp. 263–64 notes 29 and 30.

105. This term was coined by Erich Jantsch, *The Self-organizing Universe*, p. 163.

106. The story does not tell us from where the visitors come. To a certain extent, the episode that follows is reminiscent of the one in the "Hymn of the Pearl" where the father sends a letter, signed by all the dignitaries, to his son, who is stranded in Egypt, to remind him of his task. The main difference in our story is that the episode is psychologically thought through and that the youth's eventual release is effected by the youth himself.

107. Erich Jantsch, *Self-organizing Universe*, p. 196. The term *ultracycle* was coined by Thomas Ballmer and Ernst von Weizsäcker. As Erich Jantsch (p. 106) points out, in an ultracycle "the evolution of higher complexity does not result from competition, as in a hypercycle, but from interdependence within a larger system."

108. The Vinaya is meant to make us cope with *'dod-chags*, our concupiscence and sexuality, the Sutra with *zhe-sdang*, our aversion, hatred, enmity and so on, and the Abhidharma with *gti-mug*, our mental sluggishness, dullness, and spiritual blindness.

109. The meaning of this term "that which has its goal within itself" (from the Greek *en* "in," *telos* "goal," and *echein* "to have"), used wherever teleological thinking is at work (Thomas Aquinas, Gottfried Wilhelm Leibniz, Johann Wolfgang von Goethe), is in certain respects similar to the idea of the *khye'u chung*; see introduction, pp. 8f.

110. God-kyi ldem-'phru-can, *dGongs-pa zang-thal*, p. 624, understands by this "entelechy" a guiding image (*sprul-pa'i sku*) who explicates what matters in life (*chos*) to those of low intelligence, according to their level of understanding; to those of some intermediary intelligence he teaches the three sections of the Buddhist canon; to those of high intelligence he teaches the Tantras (*rgyud*), spiritual admonitions (*lung*), and spiritual instructions (*man-ngag*); to those of highest intelligence he speaks of

the presence of spiritual wakefulness in the precious citadel of one's "heart" (*tsitta*) as it is to be released (from its concealment) through four intensifications of one's cognitive capacity (*shes-rab bzhi*, see above, pp. 71ff.), so that one cannot but stand free from samsara. This image does not hold one's supraconscious ec-static intensity prisoner, for it suffices to recogize one's dynamic being (as being of the nature of) originary awareness (modes).

111. In this context, the typology developed by C. G. Jung turns out to be very helpful for an understanding. See his *Psychological Types*, Index, s.v. function(s).

112. On the idea of sheaths (*sbubs*) see introduction, p. 30 n. 72.

113. *tshom-bu*. Outwardly seen what is meant by this term is the placing of precious stones and other objects such as flowers and colored powder at various places in a *maṇḍala*. From an experiential point of view, a *tshom-bu* is a kind of miniature *maṇḍala* within a larger one as which the dynamics of wholeness "geometrizes" itself. See *mKha'-yang*, vol. 2, pp. 71, 73, 103.

114. *Rig-pa rang-shar*, p. 695.

115. On the relationship between *shes-rab* and *rtogs*, see Rong-zom Chos-kyi bzang-po, *gSang-'grel*, fols. 52b and 97b.

116. More literally and more exactly rendered "the apprehendable-*cum*-apprehending (structure)."

117. In *mKha'-yang*, vol. 3, p. 125 the term *rnam-rtog bag-chags-kyi sbubs* is used, while in *Bi-ma snying-thig*, vol. 2, p. 445 the term *rnam-rtog bag-chags-kyi lus* is used. This text uses the terms *sku* and *lus* interchangeably. Thus, instead of *rin-chen sbubs* or its synonym *ka-dag rin-po-che gsang-ba' sbubs* (*Theg-mchog*, vol. 2, p. 507; *Tshig-don*, p. 497) it uses *rin-po-che gsang-ba'i lus*; instead of *ye-shes sgyu-ma'i sbubs* (*mKha'-yang*, vol. 3, pp. 125, 129) it uses *ye-shes sgyu-ma'i lus*. To these three *lus* it adds a forth one, a *rnam-par rig-tsam-gyi lus* which corresponds to what we call the "detection threshold," or the point at which the energy level is just sufficient for us to detect the presence of a stimulus.

118. See Marie-Louise von Franz, *On Dreams & Death*, p. 144.

119. See chapter 1, p. 37.

120. The difficulty in this explanation lies with the verb (verbal adjective or vector feeling-tone) *grol* that, literally speaking, intimates a "becoming free." Does this mean that "freedom" is just another prison? This is a serious question which Erich Jantsch, *The Self-organizing Universe*, p. 210, has clearly posed:

. . . does the evolution of mind follow a predetermined pattern? Or does such an assumption again lead to a wrong conclusion already prefigured in process thinking, just as the predetermination of structures has been prefigured by mechanistic, structure-oriented thinking? Is the formula of Eastern mysticism that the universe is made to become self-reflexive, only the expression of an inherent limitation of Eastern process philosophy?

121. *Theg-mchog*, vol. 1, p. 330.

122. *dGongs-pa zang-thal*, p. 625.

123. *sPros-bral don-gsal*, fol. 47b.

124. Ibid., fol. 48b.

125. The same idea in slightly different words has been expressed by Klong-chen rab–'byams-pa, *Bla-yang*, vol. 1, p. 443: "mentation (*sems*) is the effulgence of the supraconscious ec-static intensity (*rig-pa'i gdangs*) riding on the storm (of karmic blundering); supraconscious ec-static intensity (*rig-pa*) is an auto-luminescence (*rang-gsal*) in which there is no storminess whatsoever."

126. See his *Zab–yang*, vol. 1, pp. 362f., vol. 2, pp. 382f.; *Tshig-don*, p. 336, and *Theg-mchog*, vol. 2, pp. 191f.

127. *Bla-yang*, vol. 1, pp. 441f.

128. Technically this level is known as the "arcane" (*gsang*) level in the three-level imaginative process. The two "lower" ones are the "outer" (*phyi*) level, dealing with ways to become relaxed in body, speech, and mind, and the "inner" (*nang*) level, the imaged feeling (that is the same as the felt imaging) of our body's fine-structure as it evolves out of morphogenetic information (*thig-le*) that is carried by the evolving body's motility (*rlung*) along a network of trajectories of its own making. See, for instance, *sPros-bral don-gsal*, fol. 47b.

129. A gloss explicitly states that it is "the eye [that sees] that is the way."

130. *Theg-mchog*, vol. 1, p. 330. The standard listing of four lighting-up phases (*snang-ba*) of which only three are mentioned here, is "the lighting-up of Being's (the whole's) possibilizing dynamics in the immediacy of its experience" (*chos-nyid mngon-sum*), "the lighting-up of the intensification of the feeling in this lighting-up" (*nyams gong 'phel-ba*), "the lighting-up of the supraconscious ecstatic intensity having reached the limit of its scope" (*rig-pa tshad phebs*), and "the lighting-up of (what

is the) end of Being's possibilizing dynamics" (*chos-nyid zad-pa*). For obvious reasons the fourth lighting-up that comes close to what we would call a "post mortem" experience, is not mentioned in this context. For further details, see my *Meditation Differently*, p. 191 n. 102.

131. *dGongs-pa zang-thal*, vol. 2, p. 626.

132. This passage is unusual in the sense that the "self-originated lamp" (*rang-byung-gi sgron-ma*) is related to the supraconscious ecstatic intensity and not to the appreciative-inspiring acumen with which traditionally this lamp has been associated as its technical name *shes-rab rang-byung-gi sgron-ma* clearly shows. Similarly the "lamp that presents Being's field-like expanse" is traditionally linked with the meanings that are born in it in their "pure" or symbolic character: *dag-pa dbyings-kyi sgron-ma* or *dbyings rnam-par dag-pa'i sgron-ma*. See for instance *Bla-yang*, vol. 1, p. 299 and *Tshig-don*, pp. 271f. For further details on the lamps, ranging from four to ten in rDzogs-chen (sNying-thig) literature, see my *Meditation Differently*.

133. For details and the explication of their names see my *Meditation Differently*, pp. 83–90.

134. See *Rig-pa rang-shar*, p. 559:
de-la sgron-ma rnam-pa gnyis
dbyings dang rig-par bstan-pa'o
There are two kinds of lamps;
They are are shown to be the *dbyings* and the *rig-pa*.
References to two lamps in this work are found on pp. 490, 491, 492, 530, 536, 559, 658. On p. 648, four lamps are mentioned of which the names of three tally with the sNying-thig tradition.

135. *mKha'-yang*, vol. 2, p. 399 explicitly states:
dbyings and rig-pa can neither be added up to nor subtracted from each other, they abide in the manner of the sun and its rays.

136. *Bi-ma snying-thig*, vol. 2, p. 38

137. That is to say that it shines through both eyes.

138. This cryptic statement concerning *rig-pa* demands the well-nigh impossible, namely, that we think of two contrary notions fused into a single dynamic one. Thus, the term *thig-le* means both the invariance (*thig*) of the supraconscious ecstatic intensity and the disclosure (*le*) of what becomes its cognitive domain. See *Mu-tig phreng-ba*, p. 497 and my *Meditation Differently*. The disclosure occurs in the wake of its outward directed glow (*gdangs*). Similarly, the intensity-"stuff" (*ngo-bo*) of this

supraconscious ecstatic intensity is indestructible (adamantine, *rdo-rje*), but being energy it is not static, but subtly "trembling" (*'gul-ba*) and forming interference patterns described in terms of gestalts. As Klong-chen rab–'byams-pa in his *Tshig-don*, p. 267, points out: "its "stuff" resides in one's heart, its outward glow in one's eyes." Thereby it enables our eyes to "see" actively and creatively.

139. See the very readable account of it by Danah Zohar, *The Quantum Self*, pp. 225f.

140. The eyes are explicitly mentioned as the "outlets" (*'char-sgo*) and the "site" (*rten*) of the two lamps, called *"dbyings rnam-par dag-pa'i sgron-ma"* and *"thig-le stong-pa'i sgron-ma."* See *Tshig-don*, pp. 266f. and 274, where earlier sources are quoted.

141. See also David Michael Levin, *The Opening of Vision*, p. 393 and, specifically, p. 398 where he criticizes the mystifying and/or trivializing appellation "mystical," so often bandied about in the context of what is a deeply felt experience,

142. Literally rendered this word means "the lord (*rje*) of the mineral world (*rdo*)."

143. *Theg-mchog*, vol. 2, p. 220.

144. *Ibid.*, p. 220.

145. *mKha'-yang*, vol. 2, p. 399.

146. *mKha'-yang*, vol. 1, p. 476. The same image in different terms (*ko-mo* instead of *mtsho*) is used in *mKha'-yang*, vol. 2, p. 399.

147. *Seng-ge rtsal-rdzogs*, p. 317. On this theme see also Jill Purce's outstanding study *The Mystic Spiral*.

148. *Yi-ge med-pa*, pp. 236f. The similarity of this idea with the Western medieval notion expressed in the famous sentence *"Deus (vel mundus) est sphaera infinita, cuius centrum est ubique et circumferentia nusquam "* is unmistakable. This famous sentence is the subject of Dietrich Mahnke's *Unendliche Sphäre und Allmittelpunkt*, quoted and referred to by Marie-Louise von Franz, *Number and Time*, p. 178.

149. This refers to the protective circle imaged as being made of diamond-scepters and forming part of the meditative ritual. For details see my *The Creative Vision*.

150. It cannot be too strongly emphasized that Freudians have no comprehension of intimacy. Because of their mechanistic reductionist thinking it is nothing but the rubbing together of two epidermises, and

the re-union of brother and sister in their parents' home is just another instance of their obsession with the incest taboo. A trenchant critique of the Freudians' incomprehension of intimacy has been given by Danah Zohar, *The Quantum Self*, p. 131.

151. Depending on whether you look at it from a supraconscious perspective or a terrestrial perspective.

152. Its technical term is *de-bzhin gshegs-pa'i rigs*, which, when literally rendered, means an individual's being disposed to move into the beingness of Being. It is "accompanied" by four other resonance domains, each acting as an auxiliary branch-system: together they form a *maṇḍala*.

153. It may not be out of place here to highlight the Buddhists' insight into the degrees of "intimacy," each subsequent degree surpassing the preceding one in intensity. Certainly the intensity of the intimacy between the masculine and feminine principles as luminous forces (*yab–yum*) in the "nature of things," as we would say, is greater than the one between husband and wife (father and mother, *pha-ma*) as their tangible presences. Still greater is the intimacy between the supraordinate forces symbolized as a "regent" (*rgyal-ba*) and his "mistress" (*dbang-phyug-ma*, literally rendered "she who is opulent"). Nonetheless a certain dualism still prevails. The last trace of any dualism is overcome by the intimacy between son/brother and daughter/sister (*ming-sring*) because of their consanguinity in terms of a biological reductionism. Literalists and reductionists are unable to understand this sheer intimacy/intensity. See also above p. 136 n. 150.

154. A gloss by Kong-chen rab–'byams-pa explicitly states that this as yet unmapped realm is the *chos-nyid-(kyi) bar-do*—the phase transition in which the whole of Being's possibilizing dynamics (*chos-nyid*) lights up before the experiencer's gaze and where, in Pamasambhava's words, the experiencer's beingness as (his/her) *thinking* of thinking dawns upon either. Its experience carries with it the conviction that this lighting-up does so by itself, that, as a learning process, "is not the importation of strange knowledge into a system, but the mobilization of processes which are inherent to the learning system itself and belong to its proper cognitive domain" (Erich Jantsch, *The Self-organizing Universe*, p. 196). Consequently, it carries with it both a sense of certainty as when one meets and recognizes a person one has met before, and a sense of security as when a child settles down on its mother's lap. *Tshig-don*, pp. 458ff. In *mKha'-yang*, vol. 2, pp. 419 and 425, the conviction that this lighting-up of Being's possibilizing dynamics is Being's auto-presencing is said to bring about a sense of having a helpful friend when trying to find one's way and a sense of security.

155. Usually three gestalt experiences with distinctly anthropic qualities are mentioned:*chos-sku*, *longs-sku*, and *sprul-sku*. Forming a unitary
process structure they are referred to as the *ngo-bo-nyid-kyi sku* that is
then counted separately as a fourth *sku*. It will be remembered that which
is termed *"sku,"* rendered for brevity's sake as "gestalt" rather than by its
lengthy, though more precise paraphrase as "fore-structure of our existentiality in its various nuances," is both the expression and the expressed
of an originary awareness (*ye-shes*), itself a multivaried function of the
whole's supraconscious ecstatic intensity that by its brilliance dispels the
darkness of ego-logical mentation (*sems*). In his *Nyi-zla'i snying-po*, fol.
25b, Padmasambhava gives a forceful description of the function of this
triadic-triune gestaltism:

> The executioner Self-existent originary awareness
> Tears out the real demon (in a person—his) ego or self.
> Residing in this superb self-existent originary awareness
> The valiant heroes —the three gestalts
> Tear out the three poisons —the emotional pollutants and
> Build the king's palace—the three gestalts,
> With spiritual darkness killed the *chos-sku* is seen;
> With hatred-aversion killed the *longs-sku* is seen;
> With desire-attachment killed the *sprul-sku* is seen; and
> With the three poisons killed the (whole's) triune gestaltism is seen.

Apart from this standard listing of three or four *sku* works dealing with
the experience of what is so described five *sku* are "counted." See chapter
1, p. 63 n. 23. The fact that what is termed *"sku"* is not a denotable thing,
but a deeply felt experience is well attested in the *Nam-mkha' 'bar-ba'i
rgyud* (sDe-dge ed., vol. 1, fols. 89b–100b), fol. 94b–95a. This work is said
to have been expounded by a certain Śrī-Ratnavajra, Lord of yogis.
Although nothing is known about this author, the work certainly belongs
to the mystic *yang-ti* tradition whose initiator was Padmasamabhava himself. In this work, five *sku* and five *ye-shes* are listed and "explained" in a
manner that is completely different from their standard "definitions"; it
strongly suggests that the number "five" is not to be taken numerically
but is to be understood as nuances of a single experience. There is as the
"object" phase of the experiential process

1. a gestalt experience that expresses the whole's energy in its illimitable depth (*snying-po gting mtha'-yas-pa'i sku*),

2. a gestalt experience that expresses the whole's namelessness and
   measurelessness (that is its primordial) beginning (*sngon-thog ming-
   med mtha'-bral-ba'i sku*),

3. a gestalt experience that expresses the whole's originary purity and

pure *Symbolhaftigkeit* and birthlessness (*ye-dag ka-dag skye-ba-med-pa'i sku*),

4. a gestalt experience that expresses the whole's insubstantiality and dissipativeness (*dngos-med zang-ka'i sku*), and

5. a gestalt experience that expresses the whole's (ego-logical) non-activity and its lying beyond the scope of the (ego-centered) intellect (*byar-med blo-'das-kyi sku*).

Correspondingly there is as the "act" phase of the experiential process

1. an originary awareness that is (the whole's) pure *Symbolhaftigkeit* and birthlessness (*ka-dag skye-ba-med-pa'i ye-shes*),

2. an originary awareness that radiates out of the vortex of (the whole's) *lumen naturale* (*'od-gsal klong-nas gsal-ba'i ye-shes*),

3. an originary awareness that is self-originated and radiant as a holistic luminescence (*rang-byung ngang-gdangs gsal-ba'i ye-shes*),

4. an originary awareness that radiates in its own (light) and is such that (whatever darkness there may have been) has dissipated by itself and expanded (into a presence of sheer light) (*rang-gsal rang-sangs-rgyas-pa'i ye-shes*), and

5. an originary awareness that lights up by itself and (in this very auto-presencing) dissolves in its legitimate dwelling (that is its) freedom (*rang-snang rang-sar grol-ba'i ye-shes*).

156. This symmetry breaking is technically referred to as the lighting-up of Being (*gshi-snang*) in which one pole in the ensuing complementarity is in cognitive terms referred to as *lhan-cig-skyes-pa'i ma-rig-pa* "a lowered state of the supraconscious ecstatic intensity that emerges simultaneously with (the supraconscious ecstatic intensity's functioning as originary awareness modes, *lhan-cig-skyes-pa'i ye-shes*)." In psychological terms, the self's "shadow" is always with the self. This inner tension and nonequilibrium is the effectiveness principle in the individuation process, in a human being's growth into his/her humanity. The importance of understanding through encountering (*ngo-sprod*) this inner dynamics has been concisely presented by Klong-chen rab-'byams-pa in an essay entitled *dPe-don gsal-byed sgron-me* (in: *Bla-yang*, vol. 2, pp. 20–35), almost verbatim taken over in his monumental *Theg-mchog*, vol. 2, pp. 337ff.

157. There are eight styles of stūpas (Tib. *mchod-rten*) in Tibet. They have been discussed in detail by Gega Lama, *Principles of Tibetan Art*, pp. 343–358. On the symbolism of the stūpa see, in particular, Lama Anagarika Govinda, *Psycho-cosmic Symbolism of the Buddhist Stūpa*.

158. This idea is clearly expressed by Padmasambhava who devotes a whole chapter to spirituality's (*sems-nyid*) molding itself into a stūpa (*mchod-rten*), followed by another chapter giving a hermeneutical explication of the term *mchod-rten*—"the site (*rten*) on and in which the whole's celebration (*mchod*) of itself takes place"—in his *sNang-srid kha-sbyor*. Though similar in content, the versions in *rNying-rgyud*, vol. 5, pp. 526–598, and the *sDe-dge* edition, vol. 2, foll. 204a–265b, differ considerably in diction and arrangement.

159. C. G. Jung's phrase "effective psychic personalities" (in his commentary on Richard Wilhelm's translation of *The Secret of the Golden Flower*, p. 112) aptly describes these luminous presences.

160. *mKha'-snying*, vol. 1, p. 30. Special attention should be drawn to the fact that in rDzogs-chen (sNying-thig) works *sangs-rgyas*, usually rendered in English by the static term Buddha, is always understood to indicate a process structure of dissipation (*sangs*) and unfolding (*rgyas*) with emphasis on the process. This triad of *sku*, *'od*, and *zer* occurs once again in *Rig-pa rang-shar*, p. 683. Variations of this triad are *sku*, *'od*, and *ye-shes* (*dGongs-pa zang-thal*, vol. 4, p. 249; *Tshig-don*, pp. 226f.), and *sku*, *'od*, and *rig-pa* (*Bi-ma snying-thig*, vol. 2, pp. 337, 340, 341).

161. *mngon-po*. See *Zab–yang*, vol. 1, p. 280; *mKha'-yang*, vol. 2, pp. 195, 201.

162. *rgyal-ba*. See *Rig-pa rang-shar*, p. 640.

163. *ston-pa*. See *Rig-pa rang-shar*, p. 575.

164. *Seng-ge rtsal-rdzogs*, p. 377. By rendering the Tibetan term *sangs-rgyas* in the above manner, I attempt to fuse the static notion of a *thing*-Buddha (so prevalent in reductionist thinking, both East and West) and the dynamic notion of a process structuring itself continuously anew, as which it has been conceived of in rDzogs-chen (sNying-thig) thinking and expressed in the terse statement of the whole's unfolding and self-realization of evolution since time before time and continuing into time after time—*ye sangs-rgyas-la yang sangs-rgyas*. See *Bla-yang*, vol. 1, p. 296; *Tshig-don*, p. 183; *Zab–yang*, vol. 1, pp. 225, 297.

165. It may not be superfluous to point out once again that "invariance" and "process" do not contradict each other. The "light" (*'od*) is, as we have noted before, throughly dynamic and, as the *dGongs-pa zang-thal*, vol. 4, p. 249 points out, is "in its ground state (*gzhi*) an inner radiance (*nang-gsal*) and in its evolved state (*'bras-bu*) a radiance (in the shape of) 'lamps' (*sgron-ma*)." This radiance, the *lumen naturale* of our being, shines most brightly through our eyes that by this light have been enabled

to "see." Intimately connected, if not to say, identical with the "spiritual" (*thugs-rje* and/or *ye-shes* as a function of *rig-pa*) this light glows as the warmth of compassion.

166. *mes-po*. Literally "grandfather."

167. *sPros-bral don-gsal*, fol. 7b.

168. Padmasambhava in his *gTer-snying*, fol. 316a, attempts to give an idea of it by speaking of it as a palace (*pho-brang*), as an all-encompassing circle (*dkyil*), as a vortex (*klong*), as the sky (*mkha'*), as Being-in-its-beingness in utter purity (*de-nyid rnam-par dag-pa*). There, in its unlimitedness and unbrokenness resides the primordial *sangs-rgyas* of the first chiliocosmos of hoary antiquity—Light-Invariant (*sngon-thog spyi-phud-kyi sangs-rgyas 'od mi-'gyur-ba*).

169. On this rather inexact phrase, see above, chapter 1, pp. 37, 58.

170. The terms *lhun-grub, rang-bzhin*, and *'od* are are synonymous for the whole's presence and/or actuality as may be gleaned from the triple presentation of Being or wholeness in terms of its ontology, vector feeling-tones, and (self-)presencings. See also above p. 95 Figure 2.1.

171. These possibilities (*yon-tan*) are more like what we nowadays would call "probabilistic unfoldment modalities."

172. "Mother and child meeting again" (*ma bu 'phrad*), as the texts describe this process. Padmasambhava explicitly states in his *gTer-snying*, fol. 316b that this re-union of mother and child is the putting an end to one's going astray (*'khrul gcod*). An alternative image used by him is that of "salt dissolving in water" (*lan-tshva chu-ru thim-pa*).

Epilogue

Individuation as an individual's quest for wholeness of which the two stories selected from the older Tibetan literature give a vivid account, has been the recurring theme in rDzogs-chen work. With their emphasis on lived experience as the indispensable prerequisite of any understanding of life's meaningfulness and Being's dimensionality, they markedly differ from other epistemology-oriented Buddhist texts and, with their emphasis on wholeness (*rdzogs-chen*) from a dynamic perspective, they imply that the concrete living individual is one who has lost or is on the verge of losing wholeness. With this loss the individual becomes ever more enframed, psychologically as well as perceptually rigid, closed to what for want of a better term we might call "spirit," the spiritual or the ecstasy (*Ek-stasis*) of Being/being (which in his blindness he dismisses as having little or no relevance). It is of this closure that the German poet Johann Wolfgang von Goethe spoke and warned against:

> *Die Geisterwelt ist nicht verschlossen;*
> *Dein Sinn ist zu, dein Herz ist tot!*
> The spirit world is not locked up,
> *Your* mind is closed, *your* heart is dead!
>
> (*Faust,* "Night," part I: vs. 443–444) [italics mine]

Yet, in this darkness of the individual's fragmented whole the light of his wholeness shines faintly and makes the individual yearn for the restoration of wholeness in all its brightness. In their process-oriented thinking, the rDzogs-chen thinkers were fully aware of the circularity of the processes of life that is characteristic for dynamic, complex, self-organizing, autopoietic systems of which the human individual is an immediately experienceable illustration. Circularity means the individual's linking of himself backward to the

143

source that, in rDzogs-chen thought, is the individual's luminous intensity, his *lumen naturale* or *Lichthaftigkeit*, that in metaphorical diction is his home that, as is stated in the first story, in its brilliance is of the nature of the sun. The homeward journey as the individual's individuation process, culminating in the ecstatic experience of being wholly human, is the working out of the whole's inner tension between its spiritual and instinctual aspects. The latter, as the former's "shadow," led to the disruption of an original unity whose intrinsic dynamics is the principle of complementarity expressing itself in humanly appreciable personages, be they of the same sex, as in the first story, or be they a boy and a girl, brother and sister, as in the second story.[1]

While the first story dealt with circularity in the strict sense of the word—a return to the origin, the second story, much more richly orchestrated, transformed this somewhat linear progression into an unending spiral, passing through the "origin" into ever wider dimensions. In this sense, the second story has anticipated the modern idea of evolution, which should not come as a surprise because rDzogs-chen thought is process-oriented, not structure-oriented.

Both stories have been told in response to a request by various *ḍākinīs*, semiphysical and/or semispiritual, *anima*-like forces in the whole's psychic-spiritual potential that is anthropomorphically envisioned as their "teacher," to give an account of an individual's development or individuation process in an allegorical-symbolic form that, on the part of the listener, demands the utmost of his or her imagination which, in turn, may be stimulated and aided by analogies. Allegory as a literary device has in course of time almost completely disappeared from Buddhist writings, but it was widely used in early rDzogs-chen texts and, specifically, by Padmasambhava himself who otherwise was also well versed in the use of analogies.[2]

Following the distinction drawn by C. G. Jung between sign and symbol[3] and elaborating it in order to get rid of the contentious and reductionist division into conscious and unconscious[4] by speaking of the whole's autocatalysis giving rise to our binary mode of thinking, we may say that a symbol is the self-presentation, not re-presentation, of the whole's energy-intensity in an image that is "seen" by its experiencer whose visionary capability has developed beyond the seeing of *things* into an ecstatic/*ek-static* gaze, and that in this gaze is deeply felt and immediately understood. The impact the symbol has on the beholder has been inimitably expressed by Faust whom the poet Goethe makes exclaim at the moment of his seeing the sign, in our diction, the symbol of the macrocosmos:

> Ha! *welche Wonne fliesst in diesem Blick*
> Auf einmal mir durch alle meine Sinnen!
> Ich fühle junges, heil'ges Lebensglück
> Neuglühend mir durch Nerv' und Adern rinnen.
> War es ein Gott, der diese Zeichen schrieb,
> Die mir das innre Toben stillen,
> Das arme Herz mit Freude füllen,
> Und mit geheimnisvollem Trieb
> Die Kräfte der Natur rings um mich her enthüllen?
> Bin ich ein Gott? Mir wird so licht!
> Ich schau' in diesen reinen Zügen
> Die wirkende Natur vor meiner Seele liegen.
> Ha! what *rapture* at the sight of this
> Flows suddenly through all my senses!
> I feel youth's sacred happiness of life
> Coursing with new fire through every nerve and vein.
> Was it a god who wrote these signs
> That calm my inner turmoil,
> Fill my poor heart with *joy*,
> And with *mysterious* force
> Unveil Nature's powers all around me?
> Am I a god? I feel a *light* in me!
> In these *pure* tracings
> I see creative Nature's powers spread before my soul).

(*Faust*, "Night," part I: vs. 430–441) [italics mine])

Analogy, by contrast, is a hermeneutical device that opens up a way to an understanding of the many horizon forms of lived experience by making the beholder ponder and establish new connections. That is why symbol and analogy are inextricably interwoven; what is conceived as an analogy on one level or in one direction, becomes a symbol on another level and in another direction. Both play a vital role in quickening, vitalizing, and vivifying the individuation process. Today we witness the destruction of symbols and analogies by an unprecedented reification of them, in the wake of which we ourselves become reduced to manipulatable things that have no individuality of their own. Stories of individuation, as the ones presented here, may come as a timely reminder of looking deeper and farther ahead into the beingness of our Being.

Notes

1. Freudians who have never past beyond personal genitality will triumphantly see in these images their preoccupation with homosexuality and incest. Against this profound misunderstanding Erich Neumann, *The Origins and History of Consciousness*, pp. 19f., had already spoken out long ago (1949 in the original German version). For a more recent critique of Freud's misinterpretations see Thomas Szasz, *The Myth of Psychotherapy*, pp. 123f. and passim.

2. See for instance his *sNang-srid kha-sbyor*, fol, 219 (ii) a.

3. *Psychological Types*, pp. 473ff.

4. In all fairness to Jung it must be stated that among modern psychologists he was the only one who had doubts about the unconscious being nothing else but an "entirely chaotic accumulation of instincts and images" (*The Archetypes of the Collective Unconscious*, p. 283), and he seriously struggled with its problematic. See David Michael Levin, *The Opening of Vision*, pp. 202f.

Bibliography

A. Works in English

Bachelard, Gaston. 1969. *The Poetics of Space*. Translated from the French by Maria Jolas. Boston: Beacon paperback.

Bachelard, Gaston. 1983. *Water and Dreams: An Essay on the Imagination of Matter*. Translated from the French by Edith R. Farrell. Dallas: The Pegasus Foundation.

Berendt, Joachim-Ernst. 1988. *The Third Ear: Listening to the World*. Dorset: Element Books Ltd.

Cassirer, Ernst. 1955. *Philosophie der symbolischen Formen*. Translated from the German by Ralph Manheim *The Philosophy of Symbolic Forms*. New Haven: Yale University Press.

Cooper, J. C. 1978. *An Illustrated Encyclopaedia of Traditional Symbols*. London: Thames and Hudson.

Corbin, Henry. 1960, 1988. *Avicenna and the Visionary Recital*. Translated from the French by Willard R. Trask. Princeton: Princeton University Press.

Fabricius, Johannes. 1976, rev. 1989. *Alchemy: The Medieval Alchemists and their Royal Art*. Wellingborough, Northamptonshire: The Aquarian Press.

Gega Lama. n.d. *Principles of Tibetan Art*. Antwerp: Karma Sonam Gyamtso Ling.

Govinda, Lama Anagarika. 1976. *Psycho-cosmic Symbolism of the Buddhist Stūpa*. Berkeley, CA: Dharma Publishing.

Guenther, Herbert V. 1975. *Kindly Bent to Ease Us*. Emeryville, CA: Dharma Publishing.

Guenther, Herbert V. 1984. *Matrix of Mystery: Scientific and Humanistic Aspects of rDzogs-chen Thought*. Boulder: Shambhala.

———. 1987. *The Creative Vision*. Novato, CA: Lotsawa.

147

————. 1989. *From Reductionism to Creativity: rDzogs-chen and the New Sciences of Mind*. Boston: Shambhala.

————. 1992. *Meditation Differently*. Delhi: Motilal Banarssi Das.

Guthrie, Kenneth Sylvan. 1987, 1988. *The Pythagorean Sourcebook and Library*. Grand Rapids, Michigan: Phanes Press.

Jantsch, Erich. 1975. *Design for Evolution: Self-organization and Planning in the Life of Human Systems*. New York: George Braziller.

————. 1980. *The Self-organizing Universe: Scientific and Human Implications of the Emerging Paradigm of Evolution*. Oxford: Pergamon Press.

Jonas, Hans. 1963. *The Gnostic Religion: The Message of the Alien God and the Beginnings of Christianity*. Boston: Beacon Press.

Jung, Carl Gustav. 1959, 1969, 1980. *The Archetypes and the Collective Unconscious*. Princeton: Princeton University Press.

————. 1971, 1976. *Psychological Types*. Princeton: Princeton University Press.

————. 1916. *Septem Sermones ad Mortuos*. In C. G. Jung, *Memories, Dreams, Reflections;* recorded and edited by Aniela Jaffé. 1965. New York: Vintage Books; and in Stephan A. Hoeller, *The Gnostic Jung and the Seven Sermons to the Dead*. Wheaton, IL: The Theosophical Publishing House.

Kamnitzer, Ernst ed. 1924. *Novalis Sämtliche Werke*. München: Rösl & Cie.

Knobloch, Edgar. 1972. *Beyond the Oxus. Archaeology, Art & Architecture of Central Asia*. London: Ernest Benn Limited

Kraus, Elizabeth M. 1979. *The Metaphysics of Experience: A Compendium to Whitehead's* Process and Reality. New York: Fordham University Press.

Krois, John Michael. 1987. *Cassirer: Symbolic Forms and History*. New Haven: Yale University Press.

Laszlo, Ervin. 1987. "The ψ-Field Hypothesis." In *International Synergy I S Journal* 4: p. 13–28.

Levin, David Michael. 1985. *The Body's Recollectionn of Being: Phenomenological Psychology and the Deconstruction of Nihilism*. London: Routledge & Kegan Paul.

———. 1988. *The Opening of Vision: Nihilism and the Postmodern Situation*. New York: Routledge.

———. 1989. *The Listening Self: Personal Growth, Social Change and the Closure of Metaphysics*. London: Routledge.

Meldman, Louis William. 1990. *Mystical Sex: Love, Ectsasy and the Mystical Experience*. Tucson, AR: Harbinger House.

Miles, Margaret R. 1989. *Carnal Knowing: Female Nakedness and Religious Meaning in the Christian West*. Boston: Beacon Press.

Neumann, Erich. 1954, 1973. *The Origins and History of Consciousness*. Princeton: Princeton University Press.

Noddings, Nel. 1989. *Women and Evil*. Berkeley: University of California Press.

O'Brien, Elmer. 1975. *The Essential Plotinus: Representative Treatises from the Enneads*. Indianapolis, IN: Hackett Publications.

Plotinus *The Enneads*. Translated by Stephen MacKenna, abbreviated edition 1991. London: Penguin Books.

Porphyry. 1991. *On the Cave of the Nymphs*. Translated by Thomas Taylor. Grand Rapids MI: Phanes Press.

Purce, Jill. 1974. *The Mystic Spiral: Journey of the Soul*. London: Themas and Hudson Ltd.

Ridley, B. K. 1976. *Time, Space and Things*. Harmondsworth: Penguin Books.

Robinson, James M. ed. 1990. *The Nag Hammadi Library in English*. Revised edition. SanFrancisco: Harper & Row.

Rudolph, Kurt. 1987. *Gnosis: The Nature & History of Gnosticism*. San Francisco: Harper & Row.

Sharp, Daryl. 1991. *C. G. Jung Lexicon: A Primer of Terms & Concepts*. Toronto: Inner City Books.

Sheldrake, Rupert. 1981. *A New Science of Life: The Hypothesis of Formative Causation.* Los Angeles: J. P. Tarcher.

Singer, June. 1976, 1989. *Androgyny: The Opposites Within.* Boston: Sigo Press.

Sjöö, Monica and Barbara Mor. 1987. *The Great Cosmic Mother: Rediscovering the Religion of the Earth.* San Francisco: Harper & Row.

Strasser, Stephan. 1977. *Phenomenology of Feeling: An Essay on the Phenomena of the Heart.* Pittsburgh: Duquesne University Press.

Szasz, Thomas. 1978, 1988. *The Myth of Psychotherapy.* Syracuse, NY: Syracuse University Press.

von Franz, Marie-Louise. 1974. *Number and Time: Reflections Leading toward a Unification of Depth Psychology and Physics.* Evanston IL: Northwestern University Press.

———. 1984. *On Dreams and Death: A Jungian Interpretation.* Boston: Shambhala.

———. 1990 revised ed. *Individuation in Fairy Tales.* Boston: Shambhala.

Walker, Benjamin. 1989. *Gnosticism: Its History and Influence.* Northamptonshire: The Aquarian Press.

Wilhelm, Richard. 1938. *The Secret of the Golden Flower.* London: Kegan Paul, Trench, Trubner & Co.

Wolf, Fred Alan. 1984. *Star Wave: Mind, Consciousness, and Quantum Physics.* New York: Collier Books.

Zaner, Richard M. 1964. *The Problem of Embodiment.* The Hague: Martinus Nijhoff.

Zohar, Danah. 1990. *The Quantum Self: A Revolutionary View of Human Nature and Consciousness Rooted in the New Physics.* London: Bloomsbury.

Works in Tibetan

Collections

Ati = *rNying-ma'i rgyud bcu-bdun* 3 vols., New Delhi, 1973–77

*d*Gongs-pa zang-thal = Collection of texts rediscovered by rGod-kyi ldem-'phru-can and photostatically reproduced by Pema Choden 5 vols., Leh 1973
*r*Nying-ma'i rgyud-'bum 26 vols. sDe-dge, n.d.
*s*Nying-thig ya-bzhi 11 vols. Collected by Klong-chen rab-'byams-pa, New Delhi 1970

Individual Works by Unknown Authors
in the Above Collections

Kun-tu bzang-po'i dgongs-pa zang-thal-las rDzogs-pa-chen-po sems dang rig-pa dbye-ba'i rgyud in dGongs-pa zang-thal, vol. 2, pp. 633–650
sGra-thal-'gyur chen-po'i rgyud in Ati, vol. 1, pp. 1–205
Nyi-zla kha-sbyor in Ati, vol. 3, pp. 152–233
Thig-le kun-gsal man-ngag-gi bshad-rgyud in rNying-ma'i rgyud-'bum sDe-dge ed., vol. 4, fols. 213a–278b; Thimpu ed., vol. 5, pp. 124–288
Byang-chub-sems-kyi man-ngag rin-chen phreng-ba in rNy-ing-ma'i rgyud-'bum sDe-dge ed., vol. 6, fols. 144a–168b; Thimpu ed., vol. 2, pp. 149–207
Mu-tig phreng-ba in Ati, vol. 2, pp. 417–537
Yang-gsang bla-na-med-pa rdzogs-pa-chen-po sangs-rgyas ngo-sprod-kyi bshad-rgyud in dGongs-pa zang-thal, vol. 3, pp. 519–531
Rig-pa rang-grol in Ati, vol.3, pp. 1–72
Rig-pa rang-shar in Ati, vol. 1, pp. 389–855
Seng-ge rtsal-rdzogs in Ati, vol. 2, pp. 245–415

Works by Known Authors

Klong-chen rab-'byams-pa

mKha'-snying (= mKha'-'gro snying-thig)
In: Snying-thig ya-bzhi, vols. 1–2, New Delhi 1971

mKha'-yang (= mKha'-'gro yang-tig)
In: sNying-thig ya-bzhi, vol. 4–6

Chos-dbyings rin-po-che'i mdzod, sDe-dge repr. Delhi 1983

Theg-mchog (= *Theg-pa'i mchog rin-po-che'i mdzod*), sDe-dge repr. Delhi 1983

gNas-lugs (= *gNas-lugs rin-po-che'i mdzod*), sDe-dge repr. Delhi 1983
dPe-don gsal-byed sgron-me
In: *Zab-yang*
Bi-ma snying-tig
In: *sNying-thig ya-bzhi*, vols. 7–9
Bla-yang (= *Bla-ma yang-tig*)
In: *sNying-thig ya-bzhi*, vol. 1

Tshig-don (= *gSang-ba bla-na med-pa'i'od-gsal rdo-rje snying-po'i gnas-gsum gsal-bar byed-pa'i tshig-don rin-po-che'i mdzod*), sDe-ge repr. Delhi 1983

Yid-bzhin (= *Theg-pa chen-po'i man-ngag-gi bstan-bcos yid-bzhin rin-po-che'i mdzod*) sDe-dge repr. 1983

Zab-yang (= *Zab-mo yang-tig*)
In: *sNying-thig ya-bzhi*, vols. 10–11

Ngag-dbang bstan-'dzin rdo-rje

mKha'-'gro bde-chen rgyal-mo'i sgrub-gzhung-gi 'grel-pa (= *Klong-chen snying-gi thig-le'i mkha'-'gro bde-chen rgyal-mo'i sgrub-gzhung-gi 'grel-pa rgyud-don snang-ba*
Reproduced by Sonam Topgay Kazi, New Delhi 1972

rDo-rje gling-pa

Theg-pa kun-gyi spyi-phud—Klong-chen rab-'byams-kyi rgyud
In: *rNying-ma'i rgyud-'bum*, sDe-dge ed., vol. 25

Padmasambhava

sPros-bral don-gsal (= *sPros-bral don-gsal chen-po'i rgyud*)
In: *rNying-ma'i rgyud-'bum*, sDe-dge ed., vol. 1

sNang-srid kha-sbyor (= *sNang-srid kha-snyor bdud-rtsi bcud-thigs 'khor-ba thog-mtha' gcod-pa'i rgyud*), Ibid., vol. 2

sPros-pa gcod-pa'i rtsa-ba (= *Rin-po-che bcud-kyiyang-snying thog-ma'i dras-thag gcod-pa spros-pa gcod-pa rtsa-ba'i rgyud*), Ibid., vol. 2.

sPros-pa gcod-pa sde-lnga (= *sPros-pa gcod-pa sde-lnga'i rgyud*), Ibid., vol. 2

bDud-rtsi bcud-thigs (= *Rin-po-che bdud-rtsi bcud-thigs-kyi rgyud*), Ibid., vol. 2

Nam-mkha'i mtha' dang mnyam-pa (= *Rin-po-che snang-gsal spu-gri 'bar-bas 'khrul-snang rtsad-nas gcod-pa nam-mkha'i mtha' dang mnyam-pa'i rgyud*), Ibid., vol. 2

Rin-po-che spyi-gnad skyon-sel thig-le kun-gsal-gyi rgyud, Ibid., vol. 2 [Not to be confused with the *Thig-le kun-gsal chen-po'i rgyud* which is an excerpt from the *sPros-bral don-gsal*]

gTer-snying (= *gTer-snying rin-po-che spungs-pa'i rgyud*), Ibid., vol. 2

sNying-po bcud-spungs nam-mkha' klong-yangs-kyi rgyud, ibid., vol. 2

Nyi-zla 'bar-ba (= *Thugs-kyi yang-snying dgongs-pa'i bcud-'dus-pa / ka-dag-rnams-kyi gsang-don bcud-dril-ba / ma-rig mun-sel nyi-zla 'bar-ba'i rgyud*), Ibid., vol. 2

Nyi-zla'i snying-po (= *rGyud thams-cad-kyi rgyal-po Nyi-zla'i snying-po 'od-'bar-ba bdud-rtsi rgya-mtsho 'khyil-ba'i rgyud*), Ibid., vol. 3

Ri-bo brtsegs-pa'i rgyud (= *sangs-rgyas kun-gyi dgongs-pa'i bcud-bsdus ri-bo brtsegs-pa'i rgyud*), Ibid., vol. 3

g.Yung-ston rdo-rje dpal bzang-po

gSal-byed me-long (= dPal gsang-ba snying-po'i rgyud-don gsal-byed me-long, n.p., n.d.

Rong-zom Chos-kyi bzang-po

gSang-'grel (= rGyud-rgyal gsang-ba snying-po'i 'grel-pa dkon-cos 'grel, n.p., n.d.

Śri-Ratnavajra

rGyud thams-cad-kyi rtse-rgyal nam-mkha' 'bar-ba'i rgyud
In: *rNying-ma'i rgyud-'bum,* sDe-dge ed., vol.1

Śrīsiṃha

Ye-shes gsang-ba sgron-me rin-po-che man-ngag-gi rgyud
  In: *rNying-ma'i rgyud-'bum,* sDe-dge ed., vol. 5
Byang-chub-kyi sems thugs-kyi rgyud rin-po-che spungs-pa'i rgyan
  In: *rNying-ma'i rgyud-'bum,* sDe-dge ed., vol. 6

Vimalamitra

Thig-le gsang-ba'i brda'i rgyud
In: *rNying-ma'i rgyud-'bum,* sDe-dge ed., vol. 25

Vairocana

rDzogs-chen gsang-ba'i sgron-me'i rgyud-'grel chen-mo
In: The rGyud 'bum of Vairocana, reproduced by Tashi Y. Tashigangpa, vol. 7, Leh 1971

Index of Persons and Subjects

Index of Sanskrit Terms

Index of Tibetan Terms and Phrases

(This index is also meant to be a contribution to Tibetan lexicography)

163

chos-nyid mngon-sum, 134 n.
130
chos-nyid zad-pa, 135 n. 130
chos-dbyings, 22 n. 36
mchod-rten, 139 n. 157, 140 n. 158
'char-sgo, 65 n. 28, 78 n. 101, 136
n. 140
'char-gzhi, 65 n. 28
'chi-bdag, 125 n. 62

'ja'-mtshon-can, 116 n. 6
'jig-rten-pa'i rgyan, 130 n. 92
rje, 79 n. 114, 128 n. 77, 136 n. 142
rjen-pa, 79 n. 113
rjes-'jug phun-sum-tshogs, 62 n.
14

nyag, 19 n. 15
nyag-cig, 2, 18 n. 8
nyams gong 'phel-ba, 134 n. 130
nyams-rtogs, 75 n. 84
nyams-su len-pa, 75 n. 84
nyi-ma, 22 n. 36, 62 n. 13
nyi-ma-can, 37, 52, 122 n. 37
gnyis-med-ltar, 79 n. 111
nyon-mongs-(pa), 69 n. 45, 71 n.
57, 120 n. 27, 131 n. 99
mnyam-pa, 26 n. 59
mnyam-pa-nyid, 19 n. 14, 20 n.
23, 26 n. 59
rnying-ma, xvi
snyigs-ma, 71 n. 59
snying-(ga), 21 n. 31, 79 n. 114
snying-rje, 79 n. 114
snying-rje-ltar, 79 n. 114
snying-po, 21 ns. 28, 31, 32, 76 n. 9
snying-po de-kho-na-nyid, 21
n. 28

gti-mug, 132 n. 103, 132 n. 108
gting-gsal, 72 n. 67
rten, 136 n. 140, 140 n. 158
rtogs, 27 n. 59

ltar-snang, 78 n. 104
stong/stong-pa, 66 n. 33, 71 n. 65,
77 n. 98, 107
ston-pa, 21 n. 28, 26 n. 55, 116 n.
6, 120 n. 26
ston-pa'i rgyal-po, 63 n. 16

thabs, 22 n. 36, 70 n. 50, 71 n. 55,
131 n. 97
thig-le, 74 n. 77, 107, 134 n. 128,
135 n. 138
thig-le nyag-gcig, 2, 3, 8
thig-le stong-pa'i sgron-ma,
107, 136 n. 140
thugs, 32 n. 80, 120 n. 27, 128 n. 77
thugs-kyi sprul-pa, 63 n. 16
thugs-dgongs, 23 n. 80
thugs-rje, 73 n. 67, 92, 128 n. 77
thugs-rje'i rtsal, 128 n. 82
thugs-rje rig-stong nam-mkha',
73 n. 67
thog-mtha' med-pa'i dus, 24 n. 45
thog-(ma), 21 n. 28, 32 n. 85
mtha'-grol-ltar, 79 n. 112

dag-snang, 30 n. 67
dag-pa dbyings-kyi sgron-ma, 135
n. 132
dvangs-ma, 71 n. 59
du-ma, 77 n. 98
dug, 131 n. 99
dung-khang, 74 n. 82
de-nyid rnam-par dag-pa, 141 n.
168
don, 18 n. 11, 20 n. 17, 120 n. 25
gdangs, 72 n. 66, 74 n. 82, 108, 116
n. 5, 135 n. 138
gdams-ngag, 77 n. 97
bdag, 18 n. 11, 131 ns. 94, 95
bdag-nyid, 63 n. 18
bdag-med, 131 n. 94
bdud, 117 n. 6, 118 n. 12, 125 n. 62
'chi-bdag-gyi bdud, 117 n. 6,